Prague
An architectural guide

itineraries
4

Radomíra Sedlaková

Prague
An architectural guide

arsenale et editrice

Radomíra Sedlaková
PRAGUE
AN ARCHITECTURAL GUIDE

Design
Michela Scibilia

Translation from Czech
Michal Schonberg

Photographs
Mark E. Smith

Photo credits
Radomíra Sedláková
files nn. 6, 14, 24, 36, 39, 57,
67, 76, 77, 78, 79, 84, 90,
91, 110, 112, 118, 119, 126,
131, 137, 140, 147, 149, 157,
173, 180, 187, 188, 192, 194,
205, 206, 207, 208

Printed in Italy by
EBS Editoriale Bortolazzi-Stei
Verona

First edition
October 1997

© Copyright 1997
Hatje Verlag, Stoccarda

© Pictures copyright 1996
Arsenale Editrice srl

ISBN 88-7743-160-1

Contents

LETNÁ

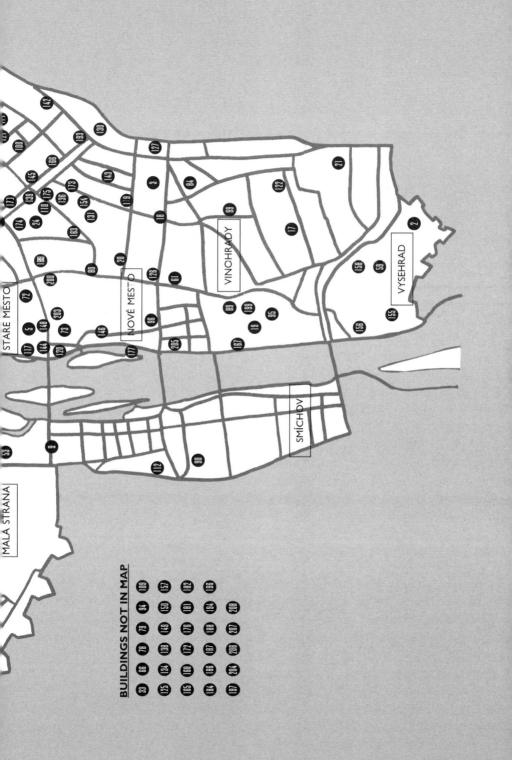

Prague Caput Regni

I.
The Church of St
Nicholas, Malá Strana.

Prague. A city imbued with the quiet magic of something intimately familiar, as if from a distant past. A city which serves as a living textbook of ten centuries of European architecture. Though in the middle of Europe, at the very centre of restless events, it never definitively succumbed to destructive influences, never underwent a fundamental reconstruction. Everything remained preserved, anything that was new grew out of something older – the Romanesque city plan, the Gothic parcelling of land, Renaissance and Baroque street façades – this comprises the fabric of Prague's current appearance.

Prague lies at an inspirational location. The river valley opens up on both sides of the Vltava – on the western side rise the hills of Hradčany and Petřín, joined to the north by the high upland plain of Letná. On the eastern side, beyond the steep cliff of Vyšehrad, the banks rise gently, opening into a natural amphitheatre, which is enclosed by another steep hill, known as Vítkov. In this setting the river creates a grandiose meander, its wide loop determining the evolution of the city. Settlement of the territory of Prague is very ancient. Small hamlets on all sides of the city were established on the higher plains, farther away from the river, in peaceful and easily defensible places. The location of the city was circumscribed by the footpath connecting the various settlements and leading to the only fordable spot along the river. In the 9th century the Prague Castle was built on the headland above the river, soon to grow into the residence congruent in importance with the centre of the newly evolving state. About a hundred years later, on the rock on the opposite side of the Vltava the Vyšehrad Castle was built – the positions of the two castles determined the future development of the settlement of

2.
The oldest extant view of Prague, taken from Dr Hartman Schedel, *Buch der Chroniken und Geschichten*, Nuremberg, 1493.

the population along the whole valley.

In the years 965-966 A.D. the merchant Ibrahim Ibn Jakub offered an interesting report concerning Prague. He described it as a city built of stone and lime, with a lively spirit of commerce stimulated by merchants visiting from all corners of the world. However, the real building growth of the city started somewhat later, in conjunction with its rising social importance – the bishopric of Prague was established in 973, the monastery of St. George was founded directly at the Prague Castle, followed 20 years later by the monastery at Břevnov. Still later a stone basilica appeared at Vyšehrad. Below the ecclesiastical buildings on important sites the city began its new active everyday life. A market place was established on the right side of the Vltava, close to the princely court at Týn, as well as two religious edifices – the rotundas of St. John on the Balustrade, and of the Holy Cross. Further to the northeast, at Poříčí near the island of Štvanice, there was the settlement of German merchants and artisans.

In the 12th century the Prague Castle was fortified; it now included the new royal palace and the Chapel of All Saints. Below the Castle, Prague was now an imposing city, uncommonly large for its time. It covered 70 hectares, with a population of about 3,500. A network of streets with wealthy town houses evolved on the right bank around the market place. Some were wooden, others built of stone, usually tower-like with two floors. They expressed the fact, that they were in a place not entirely safe, and while beauty was emphasized, the inevitable defensive aspect was also present. Each house had an uninhabited ground floor with small windows relatively high, close to the ceiling, and only a single entrance through an enclosure. Inside, however, the houses had lofty vaults seated on supporting pillars with decorated capitals. About 70 of these houses are preserved through-

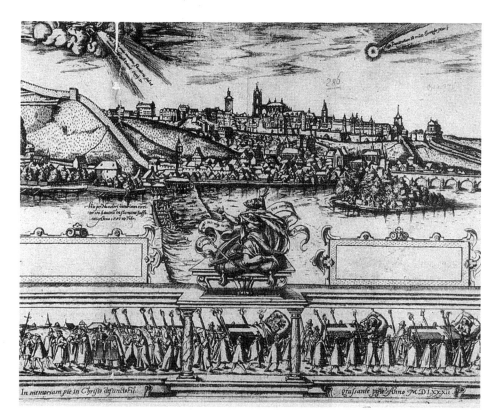

3. Anonymous, Panoramic View of Prague, late 16th century.

out Prague. Their existence was unknown for a long time, since later reconstructions concealed them perfectly. It was not until the extensive reclamation of the Jewish Quarter at the end of the 19th century that their beautiful remnants were discovered in the subterranean areas of newer buildings. The difference between the opulent town houses and the comparatively modest, sometimes almost ascetic ecclesiastic buildings was remarkable. The churches and chapels were nowhere near the grandiose dominant landmarks which are so much a part of Prague's landscape today. Given the time and the size of the city there were quite a few – not counting the independent monasteries, along the right bank of the Vltava there were 23 and along the left one 8.

The development of the city was significantly enhanced in 1172, when a stone bridge, the Judith, was built on the site of the ford, more or less following its route. The connection between the commercial and executive parts of the city became faster and more comfortable.

In 1231, the city, now covering an area of approximately 140 hectares, was enclosed by a band of fortifications 1,700 metres long, with 13 gates placed in towers. This effected a fundamental change to new construction within the city walls. Houses could

now lose their defensive character. They could open directly onto the streets, contain spacious halls, large dining rooms, and utilize their ground floors, which no longer needed to be the uninhabited spaces of the Romanesque houses. On the right bank, which rises very gently from the river, the city suffered from frequent floods. To protect it at least partially from the river, it was decided in the middle of the 13th century to raise the level of the city. The 3 meter buildup explains why the remnants of Romanesque houses were found so deep below the ground, while the street network which they formed was preserved – especially in the area of Husova, Jilská, Perštýn, and Karlova streets.

In the city delineated by the fortifications, numerous areas remained vacant requiring proper utilization. In the years 1232-34 for the first time a part of the city was established in keeping with an unified location plan: it was Havel Town (Havelské Město) with a grid network of streets, still clearly discernible

4.
View of Hrad from the Tower of the Town Hall.

in the city plan of today's Prague. Elsewhere new settlements were appearing usually with a free-form layout. In the middle of the 13th century an independent town was established on the left bank of the Vltava. It covered an area of 20 hectares, had a regular rectangular town square and a network of streets tied into it. It belonged to the German colonists and had its own fortifications. Prague was now a twin city, to become in the next century a quadruple city.

Another fundamental change in the evolution of Prague occured in the middle of the 14th century. In 1336 Charles IV became the Czech king; by deciding to make Prague his official residence, he turned it into an important European centre. His activities in this regard were remarkable. First he concentrated on the rebuilding of the royal residence at the Castle. He invited Matthias d'Arras to Prague, and later Peter Parler to incorporate a new cathedral into the ensemble of the castle buildings. The cathedral became the central theme in the history of architecture in Prague, many generations leaving their imprint on it and its construction not completed until 1929. Parler's workshop participated in the construction of the new stone bridge to replace the Judith's Bridge destroyed by a flood; he also contributed to the building of the Old Town bridge tower. In 1348, Charles IV established the University and that same year ordered one of the most grandiose urbanistic projects of the Medieval period: the establishment of the New Town of Prague (Nové Město Pražské). The new fortifications, 3.5 kilometers long encompassed a space of 360 hectares for this new part of Prague, increasing many times over the area of the city. Charles determined the basic urbanistic structure of the new quarter – its focal points being its three market squares, to which the main communications to the city gates were connected. Between them evolved a more or less regular network of streets, reacting to the irregularities of the complex terrain. The streets were established with uncommon foresight at the width of 18 and 25 meters.

In order to build his city as quickly as possible, Charles gave its citizens important privileges – anyone who pledged to build a house within 18 months would be exempted from all taxation for 12 years. In 1372 the basic structure of the city was declared completed and most of the streets were lined with houses. This was indeed an admirable accomplishment, if we consider that Prague lasted within Charles's walls until the middle of the 19th century, and that its status changed when it ceased to be the capital of a large state – and that until today it still offers not just continuous build-up, but also a wealth of greenery, parks,

13

and even prospective building sites.

The construction of New Town also stimulated great building activity in Old Town. New churches and convents were being built in the Gothic style. The new style had definitely prevailed, soon impacting on the design of newly built town houses. Especially important was the construction of the Old Town City Hall, the right to its establishment having been granted to the citizens of Prague in the year 1338. Most significant were the changes in ecclesiastical buildings. The modest and austere rotundas and small churches were being replaced by proud churches with high naves, whose interiors with ribbed vaults were bathed in light, streaming in through painted windows. Their walls blazed with colourful wall paintings and their high roofs and steeples towered over the city. Six new convents and a wealth of new churches were established in the area of New Town. The great building activity survived its patron by less than 20 years.

The beginning of the 15th century was marked by great political unrest: the Hussite movement and the resulting Hussite Wars. The effect on Prague was devastating. All building activity ceased. The Lesser Side of Prague was burnt down, Vyšehrad destroyed. A number of convents and churches within the city were plundered, and some were actually wrecked. The number of inhabitants was reduced to less than 28,000, Prague had 40,000 inhabitants in 1378. It also ceased being the royal seat, which meant it would be no longer systematically built to serve that purpose.

It was not until the reign of Jiří of Poděbrad (1448-71) that Prague again received the attention of builders and architects. The construction of the Lesser Side bridge tower of the Charles Bridge was started, preserving also the remnants of the tower of Judith's Bridge; the Týn Cathedral was completed, becoming the largest landmark of Old Town; the City Hall of Old Town was expanded and new elegant town houses began to appear throughout Prague. This trend in the building of Prague continued throughout the reign of Vladislav Jagellon, when the city recovered the glory of being the royal seat. Although the end of the 15th century was fast approaching, the Gothic style ruled Bohemia unabated. The architect Matěj Rejsek, who imprinted himself onto the city-scape of Prague by building the Gunpowder Gate (Prašná brána), influenced the reconstruction of a number of houses in Old Town. His masterpieces included the lightly rounded reticulated vaulting, which may be admired in walkways and dining halls of houses. After 1484, the next reconstruction of the Prague Castle began, led by Benedikt Rejt

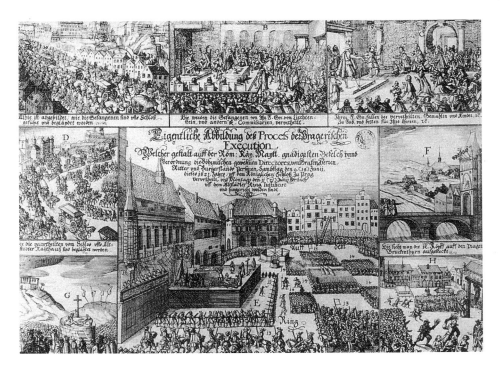

(Ried) of Pístov. The northern wing of the Royal Palace was constructed, the southern wing was rebuilt and the castle fortifications were repaired and given three new towers on the north side. Most important was the construction of the Vladislav Hall and of the equestrian stairway – a space with beautifully curved vaulting no longer following only the Gothic construction curve, but whose ribbing freely undulates and moves through space, emphasizing a sense of freedom and lightness. The windows of the northern façade of this hall are the first manifestation of Renaissance architecture in Bohemia.

Unfortunately, the glory of the reign of Charles IV never returned. In 1526, Ferdinand of Habsburg settled in Prague, paying further attention to the Castle. He had the Royal Garden established on the plain north of the Castle, above the Deer Moat (Jelení příkop). The summer palace which he built in the garden for his wife Anna was a crowning achievement of Renaissance architecture. He also built a hunting preserve above Břevnov, with the hunting chateau Hvězda, designed by his son. The Renaissance might have continued to be recognized for freestanding buildings in the countryside, had it not been for the fire on the Lesser Side, which gradually reached as far as Hradčany, and destroyed a total of 197 buildings. The catastrophe brought about an unusually fast building activity and the massive advent of Renaissance architecture on the left bank of the

6.
Anonymous, *Execution in Prague, June 21st 1621*, engraving from the first half of the 17th century.

Vltava. Beautiful palaces sprung up below the Castle, while in the garden of today's Lichtenstein house on the Lesser Side Square (Malostranské náměstí) the first free-standing villa appeared. At the beginning of the 17th century Prague still remained a large and relatively important city. It had 3,300 houses, though 700 fewer than during the reign of Charles IV, and about 60,000 inhabitants. This corresponded to the new character of the building efforts: bigger, more spacious houses on larger, sprawling lots. Prague became the haven for immigrants from all parts of Europe. The largest groups consisted of Germans and Italians. The Italians were mostly builders, masons, and architects who brought with them a new architectural style. They soon managed to adapt it to the local conditions, in which their sense of space and matter married both with local traditions and with the feeling of builders arriving from Germany. Thus Prague began to garner international character, not just because of the ethnic make-up of its citizenry. The character of the new architecture was primarily profane: the new buildings in all sections of the city often had multi-level arcaded courtyards. They addressed the streets by decorative gables, signifying wealth and comfort. While preserving their original Romanesque or Gothic parcelling of land, the houses grew up in the shadow of proud Gothic ecclesiastical structures. This was the time when the special *genius loci* manifested itself the most; in order to create and apply the new architecture, it was not necessary to destroy the earlier, it sufficed to find the appropriate harmony and enhancement: a symbiosis. Prague was becoming an international city, while also carefully maintaining a historical continuity.

The Estates' Uprising and their defeat in the Battle of White Mountain in 1620 resulted in a downturn in the city's fortune. Prague was subjected to uncontrolled looting and plunder, lasting several weeks. Within a short time the city was destitute. The political situation caused a mass exodus, mainly of the wealthiest and most illustrious families. The number of inhabitants decreased by a third, falling to 40,000. The ownership of 575 houses, 17.5% of all the houses in Prague, changed, either through sale or confiscation. Prague was to become, for a long time, an unimportant provincial city. This, however, rather surprisingly did not lead to stagnation in building.

With the Thirty Years' War still continuing, Albrecht of Wallenstein began one of the most massive reconstructions of the city. He bought 23 houses, 3 gardens, and a brickworks, thereby creating a spacious lot where he had a monumental palace built in the Early Baroque style. The proud baronial residence was

a symbol of new might competing with the power of the sovereign. After 1620, the forcible Catholic reformation of the country commenced. The Jesuit order became particularly active in extensive reconstruction efforts, both in and outside Prague. Wallenstein's resolutely ruthless approach to the original city found its followers. In many places small houses as well as palaces and gardens were being demolished to make room for the building of Jesuit colleges: on the Lesser Side, at the Livestock Market (Dobytčí trh), in the heart of Old Town. Thus at the end of the 17th and early 18th century self-contained, closed, heavy monumental city blocks were interposed onto the minute scale of the city.

The dramatic quality of Baroque architecture corresponded with the nature of the times. The victorious Catholic Church possessed in architecture a powerful weapon which it used very effectively to influence the public. Unlike Renaissance architecture, that of the Baroque became first and foremost the architecture of the Church. As such, it not only began to affect the structural ground plan of the city, but to an even greater degree its panorama. New churches emerged and many of the originally

7.
Karoly Bridge, detail.

18

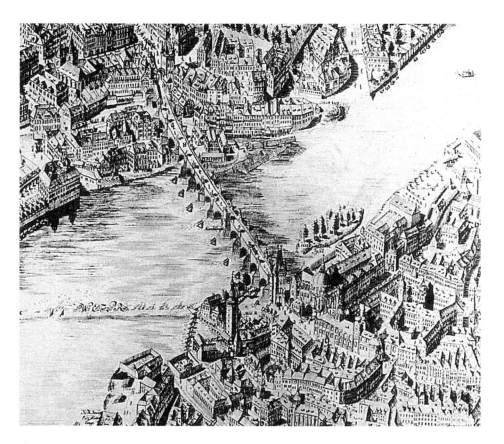

8.
Josef D. Huber,
Orthogrphic Map of Prague, 1769, detail.

Gothic churches were being rebuilt. The slim lines reaching up towards the sky were being replaced by undulating walls, massive cupolas, and shaped domes of towers. The next wave of inhabitants arriving in the city, German, French, and Italian aristocracy, who made a name for itself during the Thirty Year Wars, had acquired newly confiscated properties representing an expression of gratitude. A new series of reconstructions followed. It was not as drastic as had been the case with the ecclesiastic buildings; the new owners were often satisfied with the amalgamation of several adjacent houses behind modernized façades, with more comfortable interiors, while leaving the spatial composition of the city mostly unaltered. A new component enriched the palaces below the Castle: composed gardens scaling the inclines of the Castle cliff, or the slopes of Petřín. New elaborate and ceremonial palaces were also being built, as if Prague had not become a city without the lustre of a royal seat. It seemed obligatory or desirous for every important family to have a residence here, albeit unoccupied for most of the year since the political and social life happened elsewhere, and also to have it designed by an important architect. The massive con-

19

flagration of 1689 also facilitated a new wave of building in Old Town. Additionally, building occured outside of Prague's city limits: on the opposite side of the river facing the Royal Hunting Preserve, the first suburban summer palace was built at Troja. For a long time building was dominated by the aristocracy, but towards the end of the 17th century, the bourgeoisie became materially able to keep up with the gentry, or even to curtail its grandiose intentions, as happened during the construction of the Clam-Gallas Palace.

9.
Cosimo Castrucci, *The Prague Castle*, Florentine mosaic furniture decoration, first half of the 17th century.

At the beginning of the 18th, century a number of remarkable personalities made their mark on the architecture of Prague. These were men whose families had originally migrated to Prague from abroad, but who grew up and learnt their trade in the city and who absorbed its atmosphere and its architectural history. Prague had once again creators who managed to combine influences drawn from different parts of Europe and reconstitute them for the enrichment of the environment of Prague. Together with the sculptors and painters of their generation, architects, such as Giovanni Santini or Kilian Ignaz Dientzenhofer, turned Prague into a veritable treasure-trove of the Baroque, while still maintaining its Romanesque and Gothic parcelling of land. But then came more wars and more destruction. Possibly the worst occurred during the seven year Austro-Prussian War when the city was besieged in 1757. Though it was not captured, almost one third of all the houses, including the Castle, were damaged by bombing. Also, practically all the vineyards and orchards in the outskirts were destroyed. Nevertheless, in 1753, the reconstruction of the Prague Castle began. The diverse assembly of Gothic and Renaissance buildings received an unified Classicist façade toward the city. The defensive character of the ensemble was minimized, while its residential aspects were emphasized. The Castle became more accessible with its moat filled in and the creation of two new front courtyards. Prague must have felt that such extensive renovations might indicate the return of its status as an imperial seat. That, however, did not happen.

Prague kept growing. Not only numerically – in 1771 it had 80,000 inhabitants – it grew also territorially. Suddenly the limits of the city of Charles were becoming rather tight especially with the growth of industrial production. The first manufacturers could not find space within the city and established their workshops in the suburb of Smíchov. In 1782, just a year after the publication of the edict by which Josef II guaranteed religious freedom, 63 Prague churches and convents were closed. These included not only the oldest Church of St. John on the Balustrade and all of the rotundas, but also the new Church of St. Nicholas in Old Town, the Georgian (Jiřský) Convent at the Castle, and the Convent of St. Agnes (Anežský) in Old Town. The ecclesiastic powers were greatly curtailed, but at the same time a great architectural heritage was condemned to ruin and virtual oblivion. Some buildings were destroyed, others converted to barracks, still others were turned into newly established workshops, warehouses, or dwellings for the destitute classes. On the other hand, the dissolution of the Jesuit Order enabled the establishment of the University Library at the Klementinum. Another important reform in the life of Prague occurred in 1784. By imperial decision, the four hitherto separate towns – Old Town, New Town, Lesser Side, and Hradčany – united into a single city. The moats separating Old Town and New Town were filled and replaced by a tree-lined promenade and new parks were established on the other side of the ramparts. In 1817, the first planned suburb, Karlín, was founded on the eastern limits of the city.

The 19th century arrived with the big growth of industry which utilized the open spaces around the ramparts: at Smíchov, in Libeň, in Holešovice, and Karlín. A new river port was opened in Karlín to improve the supplying of the city. A second bridge across the Vltava was built and, in the middle of the century, the railroad reached Prague. A new influx of population occurred. The city started to struggle with modern problems, such as city traffic along the narrow streets, housing shortages, and the provision of sufficient water supplies. Technical problems began mounting at an alarming speed.

The second half of the 19th century brought about further industrial growth around Prague, as well as the necessary great

21

demand for living accomodations, first in the vicinity of the workshops and factories, and later in the new, almost exclusively residential districts of Žižkov and Vinohrady. All over the city new buildings were erected serving new purposes. The building styles were an eclectic mix of Neo-Romanesque, Neo-Gothic, Neo-Renaissance, or Neo-Baroque style, determined by the type of building and the preferences of the builder. The Neo-Renaissance style evolved practically into a national style, attesting to the patriotic awarness of the public.

10.
Samuel Prout, *Tower of the Old Town Hall*, ca. 1820.

The most important manifestation of the success and highly evolved creative sophistication of the Neo-Renaissance was visible in the competition for the National Theatre and its subsequent building on the embankment of the Vltava. Before the end of the century Prague and its image was affected by the so-called Jubilee Exhibition of the Kingdom of Bohemia which resulted in the building of the new Exhibition Grounds at the edge of the Royal Wildlife Preserve in 1891. The Exhibition demonstrated the successes of the Czech nation in the fields of industry, agriculture, culture, and in other areas. It also became an important milestone for architecture. Antonín Wiehl, the principal architect of the Exhibition, designed a number of temporary gates and pavilions, the spirit of which predated by several years the upcoming developments of the Secession style. The whole Exhibition was dominated by the Industrial Palace, with a remarkable cast-iron frame and the unprecedented span of its bearing structure. It incorporated motifs of the Secession style, set in a Neo-Renaissance façade.

The 20th century accelerated even further the changes in the architectural styles. The first decade belonged to the Secession and to its many excellent buildings, in which a symbiosis of architecture and other art forms once again occurred. Outstanding among these was the Community House (Obecní dům) which became the symbol of the success of Prague's middle classes. The style reached a high level of achievement also in residential buildings of common usage, as demonstrated on the new construction in the area of so-called reclamation, i.e. the Jewish Quarter. The area, overcrowded, and hygienically and technically totally inadequate, was liquidated at the end of the 19th century.

A special chapter in the history of Prague's architecture – actually not only Prague's – was created by the less than ten years of Cubist architecture between 1910 and 1920. Through their designs and buildings, mainly of private homes, a group of five young architects brought a new understanding of volumes and surfaces, creating a spiked, angular architecture, which never-

theless harmonized with the historical atmosphere of Prague. The end of World War I brought a change. After a long hiatus, Prague once again became the capital of an independent state. Suddenly a new political and social responsibility materialized and Prague rushed to meet it. It soon became apparent that despite its rich architectural heritage, it did not have enough suitable buildings to meet its new function. Another period of tempestuous building ensued. Suburbs and 27 villages in the vicinity were annexed to the historical city. The size of the city suddenly grew many times over, occupying an area of 24 kilometers in diameter. At its centre and in other areas, new public buildings started to appear, built mostly in historically tested dignified forms. Besides these, there were also buildings of newly formed companies, which adopted as early as the mid-twenties the new architectural style of Functionalism. After the completion of the first Exhibition Palace in the years 1926-28, the floodgates of this rational forthright style seemed to open. Straight lines, smooth unadorned surfaces, clear concrete constructions with steel accessories and windows as large as possible – how well it corresponded with the spirit of the times, which was rushing ahead to some undetermined future.

The pressing issue of residential construction erupted. The new capital attracted more and more people and the demand for accomodations was unquenchable. The first garden districts emerged, and, in 1921, the new residential borough of Dejvice was established. In 1929, the Great Depression turned the attention towards the problem of accomodations for the disadvantaged classes. Prague threw open countless architectural competitions. Accomodation became not only a social problem, but also a serious architectural and urbanistic issue. On the south-eastern edge of the city on the Pankrác plain, the first districts of public housing began to appear using Functionalist row housing and eliminating the traditional street and city blocks. On the opposite end of Prague a model colony of family homes was under construction since 1930. It was organized by the architects of the Association for Czechoslovak Achievement, a variation of the Werkbund, as an example of model dwellings for the middle classes. Houses were built in a green environment, with strip windows, flat roofs, and continuous interior living spaces. In addition, a characteristic type of a metropolitan palace was created for the centre of the city: a building with a wealth of cultural appointments in the basement – a cinema, theatre, or ball room – with a number of shops and restaurants lining the interior malls, enclosed by glass-crete vaults. The upper floors contained office spaces, with apartments on the upper-most stories. The period of the 20s and 30s of this century is usually considered to be – other than the Gothic and Baroque – the time of the finest architecture in Bohemia. Ironically, the first Prague building with a lightweight suspension wall – the White Swan Department Store – was completed in 1939, on exactly the same day that Czechoslovakia ceased to exist due to German occupation. In 1941, a building moratorium was declared for the whole territory of the Protectorate, including Prague.

The war itself did very little damage to Prague, the few air raids in 1945 hit only some individual buildings. The renewal of the city started very quickly. Some empty lots in the centre of the city were developed, but generally attention was concentrated on the building of living accomodations. From the late 50s, these were built primarily with the use of erection technology. The prefabricated housing projects gradually encircled Prague almost completely. Before that, in the early 50s, a wave of historicizing architecture, known as Socialist Realism, reached Prague. It had grandiose plans for the city, but due mostly to economic reasons, its legacy consists only of a few buildings erected in outlying areas.

After 1958 the architecture of Prague returned to the mature traditions of engineering, the search for new materials and construction methods was resumed. The houses gained in height and their volumes were simplified. The mid-70s saw the development of a new wave of Functionalism in Prague. The new, or rather renewed trend continued the tradition which Prague managed to preserve, with a few exceptions, throughout its history: the new is not created at the expense of the old, but rather through dialogue between the two, through mutual enrichment. The Romanesque and Gothic city plan is always respected, as is the historical outline of the core of the city, which is designated as a heritage site by UNESCO.

Prague is a living textbook of ten centuries of European architecture. It is inimitable and alluring by the historical value of its buildings, but also by its constant vitality and magical atmosphere, created over a long time by the mutual communication of the buildings, offered even today to anyone who comes to Prague.

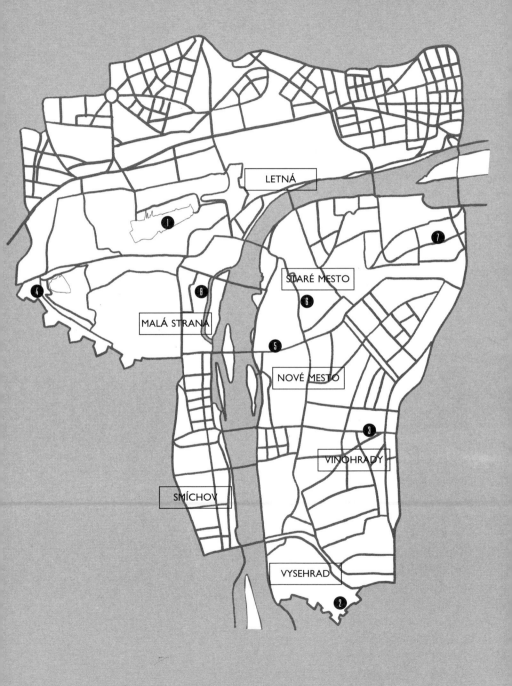

LETNÁ

STARÉ MESTO

MALÁ STRANA

NOVÉ MESTO

VINOHRADY

SMÍCHOV

VYSEHRAD

Romanesque Prague

As early as 965-966 A.D. the merchant Ibrahim Ibn Jakub wrote about Prague as a great city built of stone and lime. Although at that time such a mention could only be describing the Prague Castle, it can, nonetheless, also be used to characterize Prague's Romanesque architecture as a whole. The Prague Castle was established as the seat of royalty around 850 A.D., and from the end of the 9th century buildings were erected to reflect the importance of the ruler's residence. Foremost was the Royal Palace, then the Rotunda of St. Vitus, the Church of St. George, and the Georgian Convent, founded about 973. Somewhat later a second castle, Vyšehrad, was built on the opposite bank of the Vltava. Upon the establishment of an ecclesiastic chapter around the year 1070, prestigious buildings began to appear, including the Basilica of St. Peter and St. Paul, the Basilica of St. Lawrence, and the Rotunda of St. Martin; of these only the last still survives. This is also true of the Romanesque core of the monasteries at Strahov and Břevnov. These were concentrated primarily around the Old Town Square (Staroměstské náměstí), and in the streets leading from it. They lined significantly the connecting route between the square and Vyšehrad, today's Husova and Jilská Streets. For the most part these were buildings constructed from small cretaceous marly limestone blocks. Frequently they were located on small fortified lots, raised two stories, accessed by exterior stairways. The halls were vaulted onto central pillars with handsomely shaped capitals. These were prestigeous objects, even opulent, reflecting the wealth of their owners, particularly in contrast to the modesty of the ecclesiastical buildings.

1

Church of St. George
established before 920 A.D.
1: Hradčany, Pražský hrad (Prague
Castle) — Jiřská ulice
metro A: *Malostranská*; streetcar 22: *Pražský hrad*

The most extensive surviving Romanesque
building in Prague, part of a Benedictine convent. Built originally as a basilica with three
naves and a triple-choir closure, it was rebuilt
in the 11th century: the northern tower was
added, it was extended, elevated, and galleries
were erected above the side naves. Its current appearance dates from after 1142: the central
nave with timbered ceiling terminates in an elevated choir with an apse, under which lies a
three-aisle crypt. The side naves were vaulted and
a south tower was erected. At the beginning of
the 14th century the Late Romanesque Chapel
of St. Ludmila was added. The entrance façade
is from 1671, probably designed by F. Caratti.

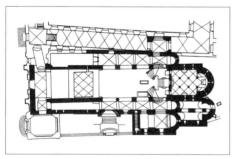

2

Rotunda of St. Martin
2nd half of 11th century
2: Vyšehrad, inside the fort
metro C: *Vyšehrad*

The oldest surviving Prague rotunda is also the
oldest completely preserved architectural relic of
Vyšehrad. It has a central plan with an apse of
an unusual parabolic shape. It was built from
midsized ashlars, with the apse decorated with
lesenes. Used to store gunpowder in the 19th
century. Restored after 1875. The wall paintings
inside are from that time. The southern portal
is Neo-Romanesque.

3
Rotunda of St. Longinus
End of 11th century
2: Nové Město, Na rybníčku
streetcar 4, 16, 22: *Štěpánská*
The rotunda was originally the parish church of the settlement of Rybníček, first mentioned in 933 A.D. It has a cylindrical nave with a diameter of approx. 5 meters, topped with a lanterned dome. Rebuilt several times, the originally regular shape of the apse was deformed by brickwork; the lantern and entrance portal were restructured. The interior contains a Baroque altar from 1762.

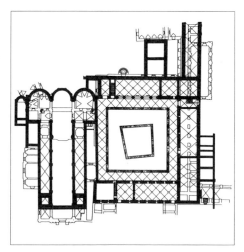

4
Strahov Monastery
founded in 1140
1: Hradčany, Strahovské nádvoří
streetcar 22: *Pohořelec*
The monastery of the Premonstratensians contains a convent building from 1142, with Romanesque joined windows preserved in the gallery. The western wing contains two Romanesque storage rooms, originally vaulted onto one and four supports. The Abbot's Cathedral of the Ascension of the Virgin Mary was originally a Romanesque basilica with two western towers and a transverse nave with three apses; it was completed in 1182. The monastery was gradually rebuilt, its finest forms being Baroque. The architects who contributed designs included G.B. Mathey (the prelature built in 1680, the buttress of the summer refectory in 1690), Jacopo Orsi (the Theological Hall, 1671-79), Carlo Lurago (reconstruction of the Cathedral, 1743-52), I. Palliardi (the Philosophical Hall, 1782-84). The Theological Hall, originally the convent library, has a semicircular vault with Early Baroque stucco cartouches. The façade of the Philosophical Hall is Classicist, the ceiling is decorated by A.F. Maulbertsch's Rococo painting *The History of Mankind* from 1794.

5

Rotunda of the Holy Cross
about 2nd quarter of 12th century
1: Nové Město, Karoliny Světlé
streetcar 4, 9, 18, 22: *Národní divadlo*
Originally this may have been a parish or estate church on the important road between the ford and Vyšehrad. It has a circular plan of approx. 6 meters in diameter, and is crowned by a dome with a pinnacle opening. The latter is enclosed by a conical roof, dominated by a lantern with dual windows. The apse is segmented by lesenes from the outside, which merge into circular friezes. The rotunda was reconstructed in 1864-65. Remnants of Gothic frescos are preserved inside.

6

House of the Lords of Kunštát and Poděbrady
last third of 12th century
1: Staré Město, Řetězová 3
metro B: *Národní*; A: *Staroměstská*
One of the best preserved Romanesque stone-built homes in Prague. An oblong palace building which belonged to a large estate with a garden, a tower and household buildings. It had two floors connected by an outside staircase. The ground floor contains a two-nave vaulted hall with a portal, to which are attached on either side two smaller halls with fireplaces. The vaults rest on massive Romanesque square and rolled-shaped columns. A Classicist residential house was built above the palace in 1846.
Romanesque houses are preserved in the basements of certain buildings, for example at Celetná 1 and 12, U radnice 10, Jilská 6, Husova 11, 21 and 44.

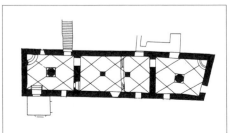

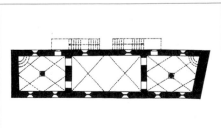

7
Church of St. Peter
before 1174
1: Nové Město, Petrské náměstí

metro B, C: Florenc

Originally the parish church of the German merchants' settlement of Poříčí. The essentially Romanesque basilica with twin frontal towers was rebuilt in the 14th and 15th centuries and expanded into the form of a three-aisle church. The south aisle is in Late Gothic style of the end of the 15th century. The church was gothicized in 1874-79 from designs J. Mocker. The remnants of the Romanesque gallery, the southern fenestral wall of the Romanesque nave, and the fragments of wall paintings were preserved.

8
Church of the Virgin Mary beneath the Chain
completed ca. 1182
1: Malá Strana, Lázeňská ulice

metro A: Malostranská; streetcar 12, 22: Malostranské náměstí

Originally part of the monastery of the Sovereign Order of the Knights of Malta, the three-nave Romanesque church was expanded around 1270 by the addition of a Gothic presbytery. In the middle of the 14th century two massive entrance towers of a planned new Gothic church were built, and then, in 1519, reduced to their current size. The remnants of the church were made Baroque, according to Carlo Lurago's design. The residues of the Romanesque building, the odd arcades, are evident in the walls of the present-day church yard. The south shoulder of the two-story Romanesque transverse nave with cross vaults is preserved on the south side of the choir.

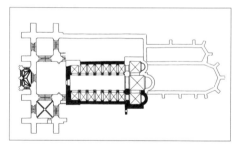

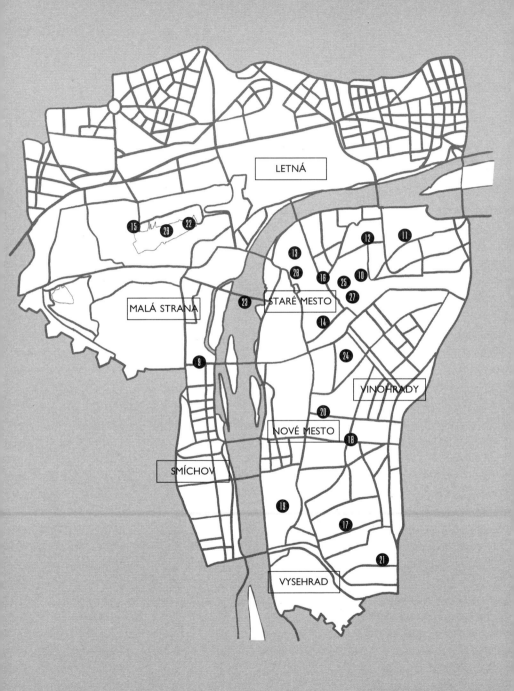

Gothic Prague

In the year 1241, when the city fortifications were completed, the life style of the townspeople began to change. The small defensive buildings were rebuilt into comfortable town residences, the street grid was logically organized, and the religious buildings afforded more space. It was through the latter, that the new Gothic style of building arrived in Prague, first utilized in the ensemble of the Convent of St. Agnes, and soon to spread widely. All the houses and churches were "modernized" in keeping with the new style. The city grew gradually: the Havel Quarter was established, then several settlements at the foot of the Castle were merged into the separate Lesser Town of Prague. The greatest prosperity, however, developed during the rule of Charles IV, who had Prague rebuilt into a city worthy of being the seat of the Holy Roman Emperor. He established the New Town (Nové Město), within whose grandiose borders Prague remained until the middle of the 19th century. He gave the city its university, started the construction of the cathedral at the Castle, and bestowed upon the city large tracts of land for the building of new churches. The slim church towers became the supreme dominant feature of the skyline and the foundation for Prague's nickname: the city of a hundred spires. He brought two important French and German architects to Prague: first Matthias d'Arras, and after him Peter Parler (Parléř), who became the royal architect of Prague. It suited the life style, which explains its continued hold; as late as the year 1477 the Old Town City Hall received a richly decorated Gothic entrance façade, and in 1487-1502 Benedikt Rejt (Riet) built the Vladislav Hall of the Prague Castle with a Gothic vault, in the style of the so-called Jagellon Gothic (although with Renaissance windows in the northern façade.)

33

9
Church of St. John the Baptist at the Laundry
1142 and 1235
1: Malá Strana, Říční ulice

streetcar 9, 12, 22: Újezd

One of the oldest churches of Malá Strana, it was the parish and cemetery church of the hamlet of Újezd. The main nave is from the 13th century, the presbytery was added in 1641-44. It was made partly Baroque in the middle of the 18th century, using designs by I. Palliardi. A hospital was established in 1662; its Early Baroque arcade structure encloses the courtyard in front of the church. In 1774 the church and the hospital were closed down and turned into a laundry.

10
Týnský Courtyard – Ungelt
end of 12th century
1: Staré Město, Týnská ulička 12 (entrance)

metro A: Staroměstská

Originally the site of a fortified princely estate, which served as a customs house, and an asylum for foreign merchants. The ground plan of its enclosed yard, with two entrance gates and houses around the perimeter, is still preserved. Houses were built from the 13th century on, with Gothic remnants visible in their entrance sections. The Granovský Palace (no. 640) was built around 1560 in the northern Italian Renaissance style with a lofty loggia and a façade decorated with chiaroscuro paintings. The House at the Blue Eagle (Dům U modrého orla, no. 643) is from the Renaissance; the Vrbnovský House is turned towards Malá Štupartská Street and the eastern gate into Týn leads through it. The House at God's Eye (Dům U božího oka, no. 634) was originally Renaissance, later rebuilt as Baroque. Its façade is decorated with portraits of three Czech rulers, Prince Václav, Charles IV, and Jiří of Poděbrady.

11
Church of St. Clement
after 1226
1: Nové Město, Klimentská ulice
streecar 5, 14, 26: Dlouhá třída
Originally a Romanesque structure, it was rebuilt
into its Gothic form in the 14th century; its nave
was vaulted only in 1578. In 1780 it was
closed and turned into a granary and warehouse.
In 1893-94 it was regothicized. A cemetery used
to be on the site of the present day park.

12
Convent of the Clarcist Nuns of St. Agnes of Bohemia
1233-ca. 1380
1: Staré Město, Anežská 12
metro A: Staroměstská; B: Náměstí Republiky; streetcar 5, 14,
26: Dlouhá třída
The oldest Czech Gothic architectural monument.
Its core consists of a long two-story brick eastern wing of the convent, with two timber-
ceilinged halls on the ground floor. Adjacent to
it is a gallery with groined vaulting. Attached to
the convent was the twin-naved Church of St.
Francis, completed in 1240, to which a presbytery with a ribbed vault was added in 1238-
45. Adjacent on the north side is a rectangular
unnamed mid-13th century church with ribbed
vaulting in three bays and the tower chapel of
St. Magdalene. An unbroken triumphant arch
connects it with the Church of St. Salvator,
one of the earliest examples of pure Cister-
cian-Burgundian Gothic, built in 1270-80. The
Church of St. Francis was destroyed in the
16th century; its current version is from 1985.
Preserved on the convent grounds is a so-called
Gothic cottage, and Renaissance and Baroque
household buildings.

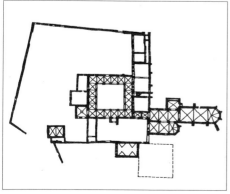

13

The Old-New Synagogue
1280
1: Josefov, Červená ulice

metro A: *Staroměstská*; streetcar 17:

Právnická fakulta

One of Prague's oldest buildings, originally built on a hillock in an open area. It is a two-nave hall with two free-standing pillars. Six bays are covered by a singular five part ribbed vault, unique in Prague, which reaches 9 meters at its appex. In the centre of the hall is a pulpit, separated by a Gothic grille from the end of the 15th century.

The sanctuary at the eastern wall has Renaissance pilasters and the original Early Gothic pediment. The synagogue has a high roof with brick gables dating to the end of the 14th cen-

tury. Low buildings were added between the 14th and 18th century. The entrance façade is decorated by Early Gothic vegetal ornamentation.

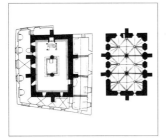

14

Church of St. Giles
1339-71
1: Staré Město, Husova ulice

metro B: *Národní*; streetcar 6, 9, 18, 22: *Národní*

The Dominican and parish church was built on the site of a small Romanesque chapel. It has a high hall with three naves of equal height, massive towers on the sides of the main entrance portal and a secondary portal in the south wall. When the church was rebuilt in the Baroque style after 1731, it received a shallow semicircular presbytery, the naves were divided by two pairs of Baroque pillars, and vaulted by Bohemian vaults. The latter have ceiling frescos by Václav Vavřinec Reiner.

15

Cathedral of St. Vitus

1334-1929

Matthias d'Arras, Peter Parler (Parléř), Josef Kranner, Josef Mocker, Kamil Hilbert

1: Hradčany, 3rd courtyard of the Prague Castle

metro A: *Malostranská*; streetcar 22: *Pražský hrad*

A Gothic cathedral consisting of five naves with a transept, a gallery, a wreath of chapels behind the choir, and three towers. Built on the site of an older Romanesque basilica, it is divided into two parts: the eastern, ending at the bell tower, is Gothic; the western was completed during the years 1867-1929. The first design which emulated the cathedral in Narbonne was created by Matthias d'Arras who built the enclosure of the cathedral with pentagonal chapels. P. Parler (Parléř) built the other perpendicular chapels and the corridor of the gallery, the triforium above the arcades of the gallery, the vaulting, and the base of the bell tower with the adjacent mosaic-decorated Golden Gate, above the main southern portal. He completed the choir and began the main nave, which was not finished. Remarkable is the extensive exterior support system around the eastern end of the cathedral. One's attention is drawn to the reticulated vaulting above the choir, the loftiness and illumination of the entire space, the rich plastic decoration in the triforium, including portraits of personalities from the time of construction.

The Chapel of St. Václav is inlaid at the base with semiprecious stones, resembling the Chapel of the Holy Cross at the Karlštejn Castle. The royal oratorium was built probably by B. Rejt (Ried) in 1493. It is decorated by naturalistically intertwined branching of ribs, joined in a suspended clasp. In the northern arm of the transept lies the Renaissance choir, designed by B. Wohlmut. Underneath it is the choir chapel with an elaborate latticed ribbed vault from 1559-61. The Neo-Gothic main nave relates stylistically to the character of Parler's composition.

37

16

Old Town City Hall
from 1338
1: Staré Město, Staroměstské náměstí 1
metro A: *Staroměstská*

The first city hall structure was known as Velflin's House, dating to the middle of the 13th century. It was adapted in 1338, when construction began on a massive tower to accomodate the City Council; then, until 1548, more houses were gradually added in the westerly direction. Only the Gothic façade and the Gothic oriel chapel in the tower survived from the original building. The western-most section has an Early Gothic vault. The rich plastically decorated façade is from 1480, possibly designed by Matěj Rejsek. The façades were gradually rebuilt, until the present day appearance was achieved, dominated by a Renaissance window from around 1520-25, with a Baroque grille from 1731. The tower has a 15th century addition with an astronomical clock from 1490. At the end of the 15th century the new City Hall building containing a formal hall with reticulated vaulting was built on the northern side behind the tower. This was taken down in the first third of the 19th century and replaced by a Neo-Gothic wing, designed by Paul Sprenger. In 1945, it burned down with only a short section under the surviving tower. Preserved within the building is a Neo-Renaissance hall of the City Council, adapted in 1911 by Josef Chochol and the Mayor's study, appointed in accordance with Jan Kotěra's designs. The exhibition areas of the western wing contain Renaissance painted ceilings.

17
Church of St. Apollinare
2nd half of 14th century.
2: Nové Město, Apolinářská ulice

streetcar 7, 8, 24: *Botanická zahrada*

A simple single-nave building with an elongated presbytery, two cruciform bays with a polygonal closure, and a narrow tower built onto the façade. At the end of the 19th century it was regothicized, using designs by Josef Mocker; the new circular window ribs in the presbytery are from this time. The original Gothic vaults and wall paintings, circa 1390, were preserved.

18
The New Town of Prague
founded in 1348
outlined by the following streets and embankments: Národní, Na Příkopě, Revoluční, Nábřeží Ludvíka Svobody, Těšnov, Wilsonova, Sokolská, Horská, Rašínovo nábřeží

metro A: *Můstek* or *Muzeum*; B: *Karlovo náměstí, Národní, Můstek, Náměstí Republiky*; C: *I.P. Pavlova, Muzeum, Hlavní nádraží, Florenc*

After 1344 the old city could no longer contain all of the inhabitants. As a result, Charles IV founded on March 26, 1348, New Town (Nové Město). Its area of 360 hectares made it three times the size of old Prague. In the street plan attention was paid to the older roads which lead out of Old Town's (Staré Město) three gates. The new streets had an established width of 18-27 meters, with the three market squares – today's Karlovo, Václavské, and Senovážné – becoming the principal axes of the city's structure. The street plan incorporated also the old outlying settlements with their churches. In key places new churches were established. By 1372 most of the new streets were staked out and lined with buildings. The city walls were taken down in four places and new gates were established: the Poříčská and Horská in the east, Koňská in the southeast, and Svinská in the south. The municipality remained within the limits of the city's walls until the mid-19th century.

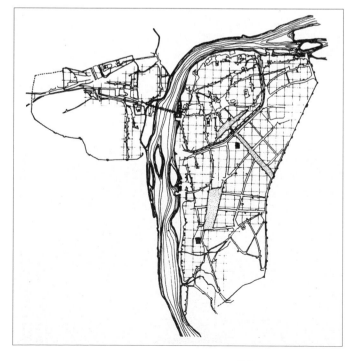

39

19

Church of the Virgin Mary and the Slavic Patrons with the Monastery of the Slavic Benedictines at Emauzy
1347-1640
2: Nové Město, Vyšehradská ulice
metro B: Palackého náměstí; streetcar 3, 4, 14, 18, 24: Moráň

The church is among the largest of Prague's Gothic cathedrals. It has three naves, is about 50 meters long, topped with a high roof with a sanctus turret. In the middle of the 17th century two Baroque towers were attached to the western façade. They were destroyed in 1945 and replaced in 1967 by a modern structure.

The monastery adheres to the church on the south side. It was originally a single story building, developed around a parvis with a gallery, vaulted with 22 bays of groined vaulting; a second floor was added in 1640. Tied into the gallery on the eastern side is a long Gothic hall, divided transversly in 1626 into the imperial chapel and the capitular hall. The western wing contains a large hall which used to serve as the refectory, decorated with Early Baroque stucco. Preserved in the gallery are early Gothic wall paintings from before 1362, depicting scenes from the Old and New Testament. The western façade of the monastery carries a mosaic painting from 1906 based on the Beuron cartoon.

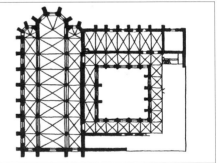

20

New Town City Hall
before 1367
2: Nové Město, Karlovo náměstí
metro B: Karlovo náměstí; streetcar 3, 4, 6, 14, 16, 22, 24: Karlovo náměstí

The Gothic eastern part of the building is the oldest. To this was added the southern wing in 1411-18, facing the square, and in 1452-56, a Late Gothic tower. It was rebuilt in the Renaissance style with high Gothic gables after 1520. In 1806, it was given Empire appearance and, in 1905, Kamil Hilbert's designs returned it to its Gothic mode.

The Renaissance entrance façade and the facing of the windows was preserved, as were the two large interior halls. One of these has Gothic ribbed vaulting on Renaissance supports, while the other – with two naves – is vaulted onto massive oval pillars.

21
Church of the Virgin Mary and St. Charlemagne at Karlov
1350-1575
2: Nové Město, Ke Karlovu
streetcar 6, 11: Nuselské schody; streetcar 4, 7, 18, 24: Albertov

Modelled after the burial church of Charlemagne at Aachen, it is an octagonal structure with a presbytery and three cupolas. The vault above the polygonal presbytery is from 1498; the central nave is covered by a ribbed star vault from 1575. The interior decoration is mostly Baroque, designed by F.M. Kaňka. Under the balcony opposite the church entrance is a triple Sacred Staircase, designed by G.B. Santini. Under the staircase is a grotto, a subterranean Chapel of the Birth of Our Lord. The church is within the precinct of the Augustinian Monastery. The building of the old abbey, originally a Gothic convent, was rendered Baroque by G.D. Orsi between 1660 and 1668. The new abbey was built between 1716 and 1719 and designed by F.M. Kaňka.

22
Chapel of All Saints
after 1370
Peter Parler (Parléř)
1: Hradčany, Pražský hrad – Jiřské náměstí
metro A: Malostranská; streetcar 22: Pražský hrad
Built as the private chapel of Charles IV on the site of a Romanesque chapel, inspired by St. Chapelle of Paris. It was enlarged after the fire of 1541, given a Renaissance entrance portal and a reticulated vault. Inside there is a Baroque altar with a painting by Váaclav Vavřinec Reiner. Remnants of Gothic architectural details are preserved.

23

The Charles Bridge
from 1357 until early 15th century
Peter Parler (Parléř)
1: connects Staré Město (Old Town)
with Malá Strana (Lesser Side)
metro A: *Malostranská* or *Staroměstská*; streetcar 12, 22:
Malostranské náměstí

It was built on the site of the Romanesque stone Judith's Bridge, destroyed by a flood. Arched above Čertovka Island, it is constructed from sandstone blocks, 520 meters long and 10 meters wide, with 16 spans.

The entrance to the bridge is controlled on both banks by bridge towers. The tower on the Old Town side rests on the first bridge pylon. It was built at the turn of the 14th century and early in the 15th, designed by Peter Parler (Parléř). The tower contains two halls, located one above the other, connected by a staircase in the south wall. The eastern façade has rich Gothic decorations, including the figures of the builders, Emperor Charles IV and King Václav IV. The decorations on the western façade were destroyed in 1648.

On the Lesser Side the bridge leads into a gate situated between two towers. The south tower which is basically Romanesque, belonged to the fortifications of the settlement from the second half of the 12th century. The taller north tower was built in 1464 and its architecture utilizes Parler's model on the opposite side of the river. The bridge railing is adorned with 30 sculptures and groups of statues, mostly from the 18th century. These include works of F.M. Brokoff and M. Braun.

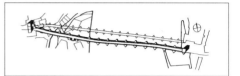

24

Church of the Virgin Mary of the Snow
1379-1397 and 1606
1: Nové Město, Jungmannovo náměstí
metro A, B: *Můstek*

Intended as a coronation church, it was started in grandiose manner, its presbytery soaring to a height of 40 meters. The actual church with three naves was to have been 110 meters long, but was never completed. In the 16th century the vaults and portals collapsed; after 1606 it was given Renaissance reticulated vaulting. Adjacent to the church is a 17th century Franciscan monastery with a large garden, currently used as a municipal park.

25

Church of the Virgin Mary before Týn

1365-1511

1: Staré Město, Staroměstské náměstí

metro A: *Staroměstská*; B: *Náměstí Republiky*

A three-naved Gothic church, built with the participation of the masonry workshop of Peter Parler (Parléř). His contribution after 1380 includes the northern portal with a baldachin portico and a relief of "The Torment of Christ" in the tympanum.

The interior is illuminated through tall elegant windows. The original groined ribbed vaults are preserved in the lateral naves, while the closures of the naves contain the original carved sediles. The stone pulpit and tin baptismal font are both Gothic, while most of the furnishing is Early Baroque.

The church was separated since its inception from the square by the building of the parish school, today appointed with Renaissance gables, which is why the façade was composed to be viewed from a distance. It has a characteristic gable, abutted by two dissimilar massive towers.

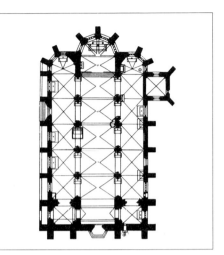

26
The Gothic Core of the Karolinum
1383
1: Staré Město, Železná 9

metro A, B: Můstek

The Karolinum began as a group of High Gothic houses with arcades and brick cross vaulting on the ground floor. After the establishment of the university college, a ceremonial hall was built in 1383, with an adjacent chapel, containing an extended oriel. Houses with classrooms and residences of professors enclosed the gallery-lined courtyard. The complex was rebuilt in the Baroque style in 1711, using designs by F.M. Kaňka. A complex reconstruction was undertaken in 1949-65 and designed by Jaroslav Fragner.

27
The Gunpowder Gate
1475
Matěj Rejsek
1: Staré Město, Celetná ulice

metro B; streetcar 5, 14, 26: Náměstí Republiky

The site originally held the Early Gothic fortification gate known as Odraná, which controlled the important point of entry into Old Town from the silver mines of Kutná Hora and which was very close to the so-called King's Court. The New Tower was built in the style of Vladislavian Gothic, using as the model Parler's Old Town bridge tower. After 1483, when the King moved to the Prague Castle, the construction of the tower was halted. Only a temporary roof was built and, from the end of the 17th century, the tower was used to store gunpowder, hence its present name. In 1799 it was stripped of its previously damaged Gothic decoration. It was restored between 1875 and 1886 and completed in the Neo-Gothic style. The design was by Josef Mocker, who also proposed the reticulated vaulting in the gateway of the tower and enriched significantly the sculptural and stone-carved decorations of the façade.

28
The Pinkas Synagogue
1479-1535
1: Josefov, Široká ulice
metro A; streetcar 12, 17: *Staroměstská*

A Late Gothic building with a hall vaulted by an opulent ribbed reticulation on Renaissance buttresses. At the beginning of the 17th century a southern wing was added as well as an enclosed women's section; these have Late Renaissance compound windows. Following reconstruction in the second half of this century, the names of the 77,297 Jews from the Czech Republic who perished during the Second World War were inscribed on the walls of the Synagogue.

29
The Royal Palace and Vladislavský Hall
from 1333
1: Hradčany, Pražský hrad (Prague Castle), 3rd courtyard
metro A: *Malostranská*; streetcar 22: *Pražský hrad*

The opulent two-story palace of the French type was built after the arrival of Charles IV, on the site of the burnt-down Romanesque palace from the time of Přemysl Otakar II.

On the ground floor it opened into the north courtyard through pointed arcades, while the first floor held two large halls and the oriel Chapel of the Virgin Mary. Around 1390, the perpendicular wing was added, the main palace was rebuilt and the spaces with barrel vaulting were erected.

On the ground floor of the western wing are two vaulted columned halls. Between 1487 and 1500, as part of the reconstruction of the first floor, B. Rejt (Ried) designed a large hall, replacing the residential halls. The resulting ceremonial hall, known as Vladislavský, is 62 meters long, 16 meters wide, and 13 meters high, with remarkable Late Gothic vaulting with interpenetrating ribs.

The windows in the north wall already have Renaissance facing. An equestrian stairway from about 1500 with a Late Gothic vault leads into the north wall of the hall. The hall opens into the so-called Ludvík's Palace from 1503-10. The Vladislavský Hall was the throne room of the Czech kings.

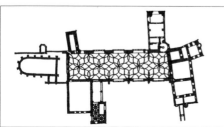

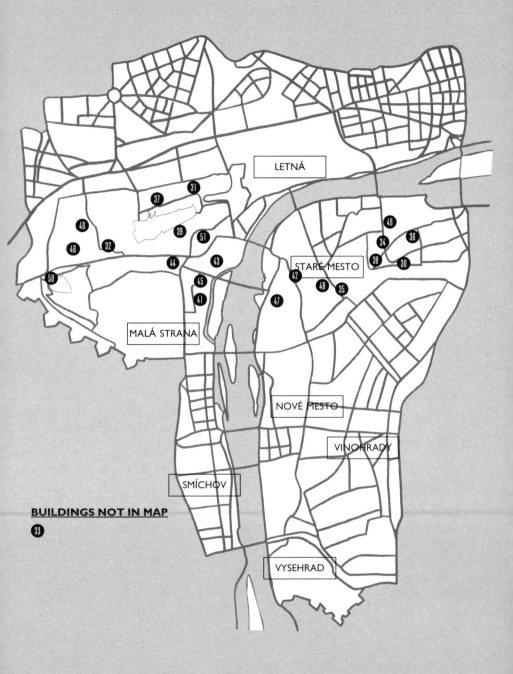

LETNÁ

37
31

40
39
51
46
32
44
43
45
41
50

STARÉ MESTO
49
34
36
38
30
42
48
35
47

MALÁ STRANA

NOVÉ MESTO

VINOHRADY

SMÍCHOV

BUILDINGS NOT IN MAP
33

VYSEHRAD

Renaissance Prague

The importance of Prague as the royal seat diminished at the beginning of the 16th century and the population decreased.
However, the city was undergoing a substantial renovation of
individual buildings, due to commercial prosperity. The houses took on a more grandiose disposition, as reflected in the new
façades. New people began arriving in Prague, coming from Germany, and especially from Italy. Several of them were builders,
who arrived with their own journeymen, and brought with them
a new method of building. However, their new houses still respected the Gothic parcelling of land and, despite all their
richness, could not overcome the Gothic dominant structures.
The Renaissance architecture in Prague is primarily residential.
With the exception of three ecclesiastical buildings, it consists
of houses and palaces with arcaded courtyards, richly shaped
gables with beautiful portals, and plentiful graffito decoration.
It does not, however, significantly affect the silhouette of the city.
The Prague Castle was substantially architecturally enriched
during the Renaissance. The Ball Courts with rich graffito decorations appeared in the royal garden, and the architect Paolo
della Stella, using Italian models, built the Belvedere Summer
Palace, encircled by a delicate arcade. During the rule of Rudolf
II great ceremonial halls were built, the Spanish Hall and the
Gallery of Rudolf, while the Church of All Saints was attached
to the living quarters of the palace. The first summer palace outside of the city limits, the Hvězda, was built in the similarly
named preserve.

30

The House at the Stone Lamb
15th century; adapted around 1520
1: Staré Město, Staroměstské náměstí 17
metro A: Můstek or Staroměstská
Originally a Gothic town house, it was rebuilt
about 1520. At that time it received a distinctive Early Renaissance façade, foreshadowing the
elements of Czech Cubism. A carved stone
house sign decorates the house, which gradually received further additions, as well as a
Late Renaissance high gable. Except for the
façade, the house was destroyed in 1945; a
modern reconstruction was done in 1948.

31

The Royal Summer Palace, known as Belvedere
1538-52 and 1557-63
Paolo della Stella, Giovanni Spatio, Giovanni Maria del Pambio, Bonifaz Wohlmut
1: Hradčany, Královská zahrada
streetcar 22: Královský letohrádek
This is the first transalpine structure built in the
Italian Renaissance style and the first time a
summer residence was situated in a designed
decorative garden. The ground floor halls are
lined by a graceful arcade, decorated with delicately carved reliefs. The second floor was
built in 1563 and enclosed by a unique wood-
en structure with rafters of a 10-meter span in
the shape of an inverted ship's hull. In the
garden, in front of the residence, is a bronze
"singing" fountain from 1568.

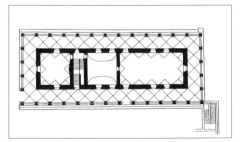

48

32
Schwarzenberský Palace
1545-67
Agostino Galli
1: Hradčany, Hradčanské náměstí 2
streetcar 22: Pražský hrad

Built on a T-shaped plan with a lateral building, the palace surrounds a ceremonial entrance courtyard. It represents one of the most characteristic Prague examples of the Czech Renaissance with a graffito façade, composed according to Venetian models. Its façade is segmented by relatively small windows and topped with a typical projecting lunette cornice from which evolve stepped gables. The four halls on the second floor have tabular painted ceilings from about 1580.

33
Hvězda Summer Palace
1555-57
Ferdinand von Tirol, Hans Tirol, Bonifaz Wohlmut
6: Dolní Liboc, Libocká ulice
streetcar 1, 2, 18: Petřiny

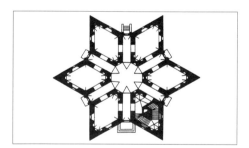

The hunting chalet is built on the central plan of a six-pointed star. Its vaulted cupola with lantern was later replaced by a low pyramidal roof. Later a sala terrena was added and a low fortification wall with bastions surrounded the chalet. On the ground floor it has remarkable vaults decorated in 334 panels with delicate stucco decoration depicting events from Greek mythology. This is the first time that stucco is used to replace the customary decoration of vaults by stone ribs. Situated on the second floor is a large central hall with a ceiling fresco from the 17th century. Surrounding the chalet is a hunting preserve with three main access alleys.

34
The Týn School

13th century, rebuilt ca. 1550
1: Staré Město, Staroměstské náměstí 14

metro A: *Staroměstská* or *Můstek*

One of the houses, typifying the architectural evolution of the centre of Prague. It has a preserved subterranean Early Gothic room with a barrel vault, while on the ground floor it has a twin arcade from the 13th and 14th century, with a ribbed vault. The upper part of the building was rebuilt in the 16th century in the spirit of Venetian Renaissance, with arched stepped gables. A walkway through the school leads to a graffito-decorated courtyard in front of the entrance to the Church of the Virgin Mary before Týn.

35
The House at the Two Golden Bears

1559-67
Bonifaz Wohlmut (?)
1: Staré Město, Kožná 1

metro A, B: *Můstek*

The originally Gothic house was rebuilt into one of the most significant Renaissance houses in Prague. It encircles an inner courtyard, with a small loggia supported by Tuscan and Ionian pillars. One of the city's most beautiful façades is decorated with delicate ornaments and carries a sign from the year 1590 with two bears. Visible on the corner are the remnants of a Classicist entrance from circa 1800.

36
Granovský Palace
ca. 1560
1: Staré Město, Týnská ulička 2
metro A: *Staroměstská*
Possibly the best preserved Renaissance town house, which today represents the western access to the Ungelt courtyard. The two-story structure contains in its courtyard wing a delicate arcaded loggia, decorated with chiaroscuro paintings depicting incidents from classical mythology.

37
The Ball Court
1563-68
Bonifaz Wohlmut
1: Hradčany, Královská zahrada
streetcar 22: *Pražský hrad*
A Renaissance building used originally for ball games contained a large interior space, 60 meters long and 14 meters high, which had a barrel vault with lunettes. Externally the Ball Court was divided by an arcade of massive Palladian pilasters; the façades were covered with rich graffito decorations. During the reconstruction after 1945, the interior space was divided into three halls, a new ceiling was installed at the height of 9 meters, and the previously empty arcades were glassed in.

38

The House at the Minute
early 15th century, adapted 1564-1610
1: Staré Město, Staroměstské náměstí 3
metro A: *Staroměstská* or *Můstek*

Essentially a Gothic house, adhering at a right angle to the group of buildings comprising the Old City Hall.
It gained a massive high lunette cornice during reconstruction in 1564. Gradually it was decorated with graffiti showing portraits of rulers, events from classical mythology, a triumphal march, and figures from the Old Testament.
A stone sculpture of a lion, from the end of the 18th century, stands on the corner. Renaissance joist ceilings and Baroque vaults decorated with paintings from before 1712 adorn the interior.

39

Smiřicky Palace
ca. 1582
1: Malá Strana, Malostranské náměstí 18
streetcar 12, 22: *Malostranské náměstí*

A Late Renaissance palace, built after an extensive fire in 1541 that destroyed a large part of Malá Strana and of the Castle. It is a massive structure built on a square plan, originally with an inner arcade courtyard. On the side facing the square it is lined with an arcade and accentuated by corner arbour towers, built 1606-13. In the mid-17th century the palace was rebuilt in the Baroque style, with another floor added, and topped with a segmented gable above the central buttress. The designer was Josef Jager.

40

The Martinitz Palace
after 1570
1: Hradčany, Hradčanské náměstí 8
streetcar 22: Brusnice

A spacious palace with an inner courtyard, built on a very irregular corner lot. Originally it had three wings and opened into a garden above a moat known as Jelení příkop. It had elaborately fashioned Renaissance gables with graffito decorations both on the outside and facing the courtyard. After 1618 a terminating tract above the garden was added.

Its composition emulates at half scale the old Royal Palace of the Prague Castle, both in the extension of the short wing over the moat, as well as by the arrangement of the interior spaces. Dominant among these is a first floor hall, with an adjacent small palace chapel.

The hall contains a ceiling of painted oval coffers, the entrance of the chapel is decorated with paintings of Adam and Eve, after Dürer. The palace also contains several painted Renaissance joist ceilings.

41

Hrzánovský Palace of the Met-tych of Čečov
1586
1: Malá Strana, Velkopřevorské náměstí 1
streetcar 12, 22: Malostranské náměstí

The sprawling, ruggedly proportioned Renaissance palace surrounds on three sides a small ceremonial courtyard. The portal, leading into the courtyard, manifests clear Northern influences, with massive bossage and a dynamically split vault head.

In its variously formed masses one can follow its many reconstructions, the last of which, in 1750, gave the wing above Čertovka its Baroque appearance.

42

The Italian Chapel of the Assumption of the Virgin Mary
1590-97
Ottorino Mascarino (?)
1: Staré Město, Karlova ulice
metro A: *Staroměstská*

The oval Renaissance building has an exterior with a lantern-topped cupola, built for the Italian residents of Prague. A Baroque portico in front of the door was designed in 1715 by František Maximilián Kaňka, who was also the author of the beautiful forged grillwork. Above the stairs the portico is turned at a right angle to cover the entrance to the Baroque Church of St. Clement in the Klementinum.

43

The House at the Three Ostriches
1597
1: Malá Strana, U lužického semináře 1
metro A: *Malostranská*; streetcar 12, 22: *Malostranské náměstí*

The Renaissance town house carries on its southern façade remnants of a painting from 1606, depicting three ostriches. In 1657 another floor was added to the building and it was given characteristic voluted Early Baroque gables. Richly painted joisted ceilings are preserved inside.

44

Vrtbovský House
1597 and 1631
1: Malá Strana, Karmelitská 25
streetcar 12, 22: *Malostranské náměstí*

A spacious Renaissance palace-like town house with a long courtyard. A terraced garden was created on the site of a former vineyard as termination of the courtyard. It was designed by F.M. Kaňka in 1720, while Matthias Braun provided both the sculptural decoration and the Atlas figure at the gate of the courtyard. The vault of the sala terrena is decorated with paintings by V.V. Reiner.

45

The Grand Priory Mill

1597-98

1: Malá Strana, Velkopřevorské náměstí 8

streetcar 12, 22: *Malostranské náměstí*

The mill is mentioned as early as 1400, when it belonged to the commendam of the Order of the Knights of St. John. In its present appearance it is a prominent feature in the panorama of the Lesser Side, especially noticeable by its high roof, originally used for storage. It is the last preserved mill on the Čertovka shoulder of the river Vltava.

46

Hradčany Town Hall

1598

Kašpar Oemichen of Oberheim

1: Hradčany, Loretánská 1

streetcar 22: *Pohořelec*

A Renaissance building on an L-shaped plan, with two unequal wings, which control the access from the street to the Hradčany Square. Placed in the corner is a massive bossed entrance portal. The higher, three-story wing has a façade completely covered with trompe-l'oeil diamond-point graffito. Preserved among these are remnants of the imperial emblem and that of Hradčany. The building is topped with uneven, perpendicularly attached volute gables.

47

The House at the Golden Well

ca.1600

1: Staré Město, Karlova 3

metro A: *Staroměstská*

A Renaissance town house which has in its inner courtyard galleries seated on stone consoles. The façade, rebuilt around 1700 in Early Baroque style, has stucco relief decoration with figures of household saints and protectors against pestilence.

48
Teyfel's House
after 1603
1: Staré Město, Melantrichova 12

metro A, B: Můstek

A town house with a passageway and an inner courtyard, encircled by Late Renaissance arcades. The outer façade is Baroque, designed possibly by František Ignác Prée, with a preserved Early Baroque portal in the style of Vignola.

49
Church of St. Salvator
1611-14
Hans Krystofel von Graubunden
1: Josefov, Salvátorská

metro A: Staroměstská; streetcar 17: Právnická fakulta

A lofty three-aisled Gothico-Renaissance structure, built for the German Lutherans.
In 1626 it was acquired by the Paulines who connected the church with their monastery on Staroměstské náměstí by means of a covered hallway. After a fire in 1689, the church was rebuilt in the Baroque style and stands were added above the side naves. Around 1720 a tower was built and the mid-18th century saw the addition of Rococo stuccos in the main nave and presbytery. In 1784 the monastery, including the church, was closed and turned into a mint. Since 1863 it belongs, once again, to the Lutherans.

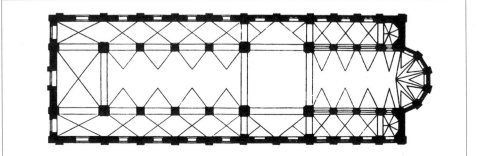

50
Church of St. Roch
1602-12
Giovanni Maria Filippi
1: Hradčany, Strahovské nádvoří
streetcar 22: *Pohořelec*
A Gothic and Renaissance central building with a cruciform plan, erected in gratitude for averting the plague of 1599. The stone details in Gothic style were created by Giacomo Bossi da Campione. The church was closed in 1784. When it was reopened 100 years later, it was adorned with three altars with terracotta statues. Today it is used as an exhibition hall.

51
The Lesser Side Town Hall
1617-19
Giovanni Maria Filippi
1: Malá Strana, Malostranské náměstí 25
streetcar 12, 22: *Malostranské náměstí*
The Late Renaissance building was created by the reconstruction of an originally Gothic house. Baroque adaptations were made in the mid-17th century. The ground floor is penetrated by an arcade with massive bossed pilasters, the portal with the town emblem is preserved, the first and second floors have windows with prominent open-work suprafenestral gables and plastically accentuated slim pilasters. The original shape of the roof attic with a corner tower and voluted gable is preserved only in the lateral façade. The towers and gables facing the square were taken down in 1822.

The interior contains a Rococo staircase and vaulted rooms, one decorated with paintings. The doors of the building were moved to the second floor of the Old Town City Hall.

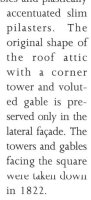

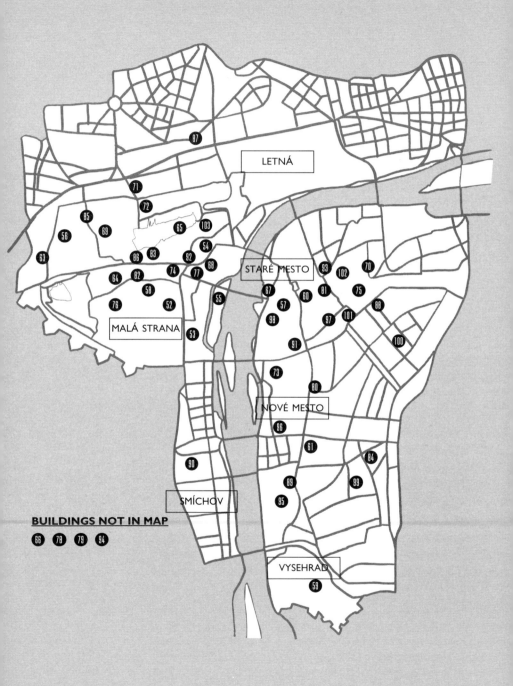

LETNÁ

87

71

72

85

56 69 65 103

54

63 86 83 92

STARÉ MESTO 93 102 70

64 82 74 77 68

58 67 60 81 75

76 52 55 57 98 97 101 88

MALÁ STRANA 53 91 100

73

80

NOVÉ MESTO

96

61

90 84

SMÍCHOV 89 99

95

BUILDINGS NOT IN MAP

66 78 79 94

VYSEHRAD

59

Baroque Prague

The Romanesque and Gothic periods gave Prague its network of streets and the elegant dominants of its spires, while the Renaissance left it with the imposing façades of its townhouses. However, its true architectural expression is first and foremost Baroque. After 1627 the Czech lands went through a period of forcible Catholic reformation, which manifested itself by a massive wave of construction of new churches, convents and monastic colleges. The influx of many new wealthy inhabitants into Prague meant the erection of a number of ostentatious palaces built in the new style, which was imported from Italy and Germany. This was first promulgated by the newly arrived architects and builders, but then adopted by local builders, including the descendants of the foreign architects, now living in Prague. Most prominent among these were the Dientzenhofers, the Luragos, and the Santinis. Like the Gothic earlier, the Baroque became the next great architectural style, and it conquered not only Prague, but all of Bohemia as well. Baroque buildings are scattered all over Prague, including the outlying suburbs; besides the city palaces, villas and chateaus were being built beyond the city limits, while the clergy erected churches for pilgrimage and new monasteries. New buildings were not the only ones affected, the new style also significantly intruded into the existing urban structure: in order to build the Jesuit College of Klementinum, a large segment of the Old Town was torn down, while a substantial part of the Lesser Side had to yield to the Wallenstein Palace. And yet, the Prague Baroque is not deafeningly ostentatious. Since its key buildings were built by architects who grew up in Prague, they managed to absorb perfectly the characteristic atmosphere of the city, and maintain its inimitable *genius loci*.

52
Church of the Virgin Mary Victorious (originally Holy Trinity)
1611-12
Giovanni Maria Filippi
1: Malá Strana, Karmelitská ulice
streetcar 12, 22: *Karmelitská or Malostranské náměstí*

The first Prague building in the Baroque spirit, is a large hall space of the Roman type, with odd arcades along the side walls. Built originally by the Lutherans, its façade was oriented westward. After 1620 it was acquired by the Barefoot Carmelites, who had it rebuilt, changing the orientation of the church relative to the street. They also moved the altar to the west and added a new monumental façade. In 1669 they built a tower onto the new presbytery. Under the church are catacombs. The low entrance terrace with a balustrade is from the mid-19th century. Adjacent to the church is the area of the former convent, now in Late Classicist style, built in 1837-39.

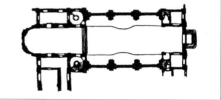

53
The Palace of the Michů z Vacínova
1623 and 1640-50
Francesco Caratti, Pietro Colombo Zaccaria Giovanni Campione de Bossi
1: Malá Strana, Újezd 40
streetcar 12, 22: *Hellichova*

At the core of the extensive palace is a small summer residence from 1580, the work of Giovanni Aostalis. Built onto its eastern side is an Early Baroque Palace with a portal.
Added subsequently was a garden wing with a massive buttress. It brought to Prague a type of Italian villa, whose architecture, with its unusual, horizontally and vertically segmented elaborate façade, was new to the city. The interior of the main hall has a vault decorated richly with stucco by Domenico Galli.

54
Wallenstein Palace
1623-30
Andrea Spezza, Nicolò Sebregondi, Giovanni Pieroni
1: Malá Strana, Valdštejnské náměstí 4

metro A: *Malostranská*; streetcar 12, 22: *Malostranské náměstí*

The extensive palace area represents the first monumental building in Prague, which shows the interpenetration of elements of the Late Renaissance and those of the Early Baroque. It was built as a prestigious residence on the former site of 23 houses, a brickworks, and a garden. The 60 meters long front of the principal palace building is opened towards the square. It is evenly divided by identical windows in three rows one above another and by three massive portals, of which the middle one is blind. Inside, behind the front, is a two-story high Knights' Hall (Rytířský sál) with a large ceiling fresco. The palace also has a large garden, lined with domestic buildings, terminated by a riding school. The garden is separated from the living quarters by a tall sala terrena, modelled after the portico of a Livornese church with rich stucco decoration. Nearby there is a bird sanctuary with a man-made cave. The architecturally conceived garden is intersected by an alley lined with

copies of sculptures of classical deities, and of horses by Adrien deVries. The originals have been in Sweden since 1648.

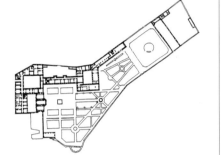

55
Lichtenstein (Kaiserstein) Palace
1684-1696
Giovanni Battista Alliprandi (?)
1: Malá Strana, U Sovových mlýnů 4

metro A: *Malostranská*; streetcar 12, 22: *Malostranské náměstí*

Originally a single story Early Baroque palace at the banks of the Vltava river, built on a hexagonal plan along an inner courtyard, with two towers terminated by gazebos. It was subject to several reconstructions, including a Neo-Classicist one in 1831, and another in the Neo-Renaissance style in 1864. Only a pillared portal survived from its Baroque appearance.

56

Loreta
1626, 1711-25 and 1746-51
Giovanni Battista Orsi, Christoph Dientzenhofer,
Kilian Ignaz Dientzenhofer
1: Hradčany, Loretánské náměstí
streetcar 22: *Pohořelec*

The extensive Baroque complex is in a place of pilgrimage, at the centre of which stands a copy of the cottage of the Virgin Mary; originally painted, it was richly decorated with stuccos in the mid-18th century. The galleries contain seven chapels: those in the centre of the north and south galleries were designed by Christoph Dientzenhofer, who also established the Church of the Birth of Our Lord (kostel Narození

Páně) in the eastern gallery. The altar painting is by Václav Vavřinec Reiner.

In 1721 Christoph Dientzenhofer built the High Baroque façade, possibly the most valuable architectural component of the ensemble. Incorporated into it is a tower with a carillon from 1694, and a modified entrance terrace with sculptures by Ondřej Quitainer. The galleries were rebuilt and raised by an additional floor in 1746.

57

Church of St. Salvator at the Klementinum
1578-1660
Carlo Lurago, Francesco Caratti
1: Staré Město, Křižovnické náměstí
metro A; streetcar 17, 18: *Staroměstská*

One of the finest Early Baroque Prague churches was built in several phases. A presbytery and a transverse nave were first built on the plan of a Renaissance basilica, followed by a triple nave with a marble portal, and galleries above the side naves. Raised above the intersection of the naves is a polygonal cupola with stucco ornamentation. It was likely designed by F. Caratti, as was the triplanar portico with the sculptures of Church Fathers, facing the square. Towers were erected at the beginning of the 18th century and the whole church was raised according to the design of F.M. Kaňka. The interior impresses with its spaciousness, airiness, and its wealth of stucco ornamentation.

58
Schönborn Palace (Colloredo)
1643-56, ca. 1715
Giovanni Santini (?)
1: Malá Strana, Tržiště 15
streetcar 12, 22: *Malostranské náměstí*

Only the carved doors of the entrance portal survive today from the original Early Baroque palace, built on the site of five older houses. Santini completely rebuilt the sprawling palace,

keeping its division into two parts. Each of these has a distinctive central buttress with a different entrance portal, whose lavish plastic framing is topped by a high dormer with an uniquely designed gable. He also emphasized the gables above the first floor windows. The carriage way is decorated on the inside with sculptures of Titans by Matthias Braun. Behind the street tract, where the palace develops in three perpendicular wings, a terraced garden rises towards the Petřín hillsides. It is crowned by a gazebo, created by the reconstruction of an old vineyard cottage in the second half of the 19th century.

59
The Baroque Fortifications at Vyšehrad
1654-78
Giovanni Battista Pieroni, Carlo Lurago, Santino Bossi
2. Vyšehrad
metro C: *Vyšehrad*

After the Thirty Year Wars it was decided to strengthen all of Prague's fortifications and to create a citadel at Vyšehrad. The old battlements were torn down to facilitate construction. The new fortifications with six massive bastions encircled all of the Vyšehrad hill, with access allowed only through two imposing gates, built one behind the other. The outer Early Baroque one with embrasures is the Tábor Gate. The inner one, the Leopold's Gate, was built in the style of Northern Italian fortification architecture of the Early Baroque Classicism. The resolution is clearly inspired by the Matyáš Gate of the Prague Castle.

60
Klementinum
1653-1770

Carlo Lurago, Francesco Caratti, Giovanni Domenico Orsi, František Maxmilián Kaňka

1: Staré Město, Křižovnické náměstí 4

metro A; streetcar 17, 18: *Staroměstská*

The third largest building complex of historical Prague was built as the principal Jesuit college in Bohemia, on land that formerly accomodated more than 30 houses, 3 churches, a convent, and a garden. The oldest and architecturally most important is the western part. It was originally two-storied, segmented by massive bossed pilasters of a high order, with stucco heads of emperors. The superstructure with dormers is from 1924-25.

The main entrance is through the portal next to the Church of St. Salvator. The college then develops around five courtyards, the oldest of which is surrounded by a gallery. An astronomical tower rises above the third courtyard. The ensemble of the Klementinum incorporates the large hall of the summer refectory with or-

nate stuccos, followed by the Mirror Chapel, also adorned with stuccos. Above is the Baroque library hall, decorated with illusionistic paintings in the cupola and appointed with Baroque furnishings. Most of the other preserved Baroque spaces (the Hall of Mathematics, Mozart's Hall, the Music Hall, etc.), have stucco ceilings with frescoes. In the 1920s the Klementinum was adapted to suit the needs of the National Library, with designs by L. Machon.

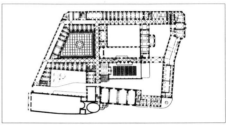

61
Church of St. Ignatius
1665-78
Carlo Lurago, Martin Reiner
2: Nové Město, Karlovo náměstí

metro B; streetcar 3, 4, 6, 7, 14, 18, 22, 24: *Karlovo náměstí*

Church with the typical Jesuit arrangements: the main hall with its shallow presbytery and an extensive sacristy is fringed by side chapels with galleries. The interior is richly adorned with frescos and stuccos, and furnished in the Baroque and Rococo styles. Characteristic is the monumentally massive façade with the statue of St. Ignatius above the entrance. The portico was added in 1697-99; it was designed by P. Bayer, who was also responsible for the church tower. Adjacent to the church stands the Early Baroque New Town Jesuit College, began in 1658 from the designs of C. Lurago, and completed in 1710 by J.J. Wirch.

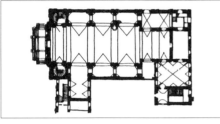

62
The Archbishop's Palace
1561, 1669-94 and 1764-65
Jean-Baptiste Mathey, Jan Josef Wirch
1: Hradčany, Hradčanské náměstí 16

streetcar 22: *Pražský hrad*

Originally a Renaissance house, adapted to the needs of the bishopric by Ulrico Aostali. A chapel with ceiling paintings and stuccos was established in 1599. During its reconstruction, Jean-Baptiste Mathey brought to Prague a new approach to the palace façade, with a high central buttress, crowned above the roof by an arbour. The reconstruction in the second half of the 18th century gave the palace the Rococo appearance with a more playful decor. Added to the palace were two lateral beamed bays with carriage ways, while the roof was united by an attic balustrade.

63
Čzernín Palace
1669-92
Francesco Caratti
1: Hradčany Loretánské náměstí 5
streetcar 22: *Pohořelec*

A monumental Early Baroque building with elements of Palladian Renaissance. The 150 meters long front façade is segmented by 30 pilasters of a high order, seated on massively bossed pediments. The northern façade is turned towards a landscaped terraced garden, with a gazebo and two sala terrenas, also in the Palladian tradition. The palace was rebuilt often, the first time in 1718-20 by František Maxmilian Kaňka. He created the inner monumental stair-way, topped with a polygonal tambour; the fresco "The Fall of Titans" by Václav Vavřinec Reiner decorated the vaulting. In 1851 the palace was damaged while being converted into barracks. It was returned to its original appearance after the reconstruction of 1928-32, designed by Pavel Janák.

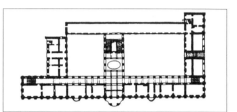

64
The House at the Two Suns
1673
1: Malá Strana, Nerudova 47
streetcar 12, 22: *Malostranské náměstí*

One of the Early Baroque town houses, two-storied, with two voluted gables, characteristic of Nerudova Street.

65
Ledeburg Palace (Trauttmansdorf)
1669, 1717 and 1787
Giovanni Santini, Giovanni Battista Alliprandi,
Ignaz Palliardi
1: Malá Strana, Valdštejnské náměstí 3
metro A: Malostranská; streetcar 12, 22: Malostranské náměstí
The palace was created by joining two Renaissance houses. Of these a single portal survived. Santini is credited with the establishment, at the end of the 17th century, of one of the most beautiful terraced gardens on the slopes below the Castle. The sala terrena on the first terrace is the work of Alliprandi. Set against a concave background, it is divided into three parts and the central one is convexly arched, with a high segmented arcade.

66
The Troja Chateau
1679-85
Jean-Baptiste Mathey
8: Troja, U trojského zámku 6
bus 112: Troja Zoo
One of the first Prague summer residences, built in the style of a suburban Roman villa. The three-winged building has a dominant higher central section, whose principal hall is richly decorated by ceiling and wall paintings. It is connected to the garden by a monumental staircase built on an oval plan.
There is a grotto under the staircase decorated by the Heerman brothers' plastics *The Defeat of the Titans by the Olympians*. The short lateral wings have notable rising stairway towers. A land-scaped garden, redesigned in 1990 by O. Kuča, is adjacent to the palace.

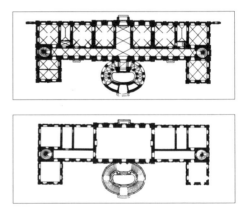

67

Church of St. Francis with the Monastery of the Knights of the Cross with the Red Star
1679-89
Jean-Baptiste Mathey, Domenico Canevalle
1: Staré Město, Křižovnické náměstí

metro A; streetcar 17, 18: *Staroměstská*

The church completed the composition of the small square approaching the Charles Bridge. It was built at the time when the massive Klementinum was already completed, the Church of St. Salvator had a new portico, and only a small space was left at the corner of the monastery of the Knights of the Cross. The church has a central plan, its vaulting, with a high robustly segmented tambour, extends above an oval plan. It is situated in an unusual north-south direction, with access through a southern entrance via a small portal leading into a shallow ante-room. A chamber space evolves from the latter, with walls segmented by marble pilasters; the niches between the pilasters harbour stucco figures of saints. The vault contains a fresco by V.V. Reiner. The presbytery, deeper than the ante-room,

is decorated by frescos by J.K. Liška. Adjacent to the church is the precinct of the monastery, consisting of, towards the square and the river, a simple Early Baroque building by C. Lurago; towards the street it consists of the monastery building from 1910-12, by J. Sakař.

68

Church of St. Josef
1686-92
Donát Ignác a Jesu
1: Malá Strana, Josefská ulice

streetcar 12, 22: *Malostranské náměstí*

Built as the final stage of the precinct of the Carmelite convent, closed in 1782. It is vaulted above an oval floor plan and lined by niches with oratories. The façade is Early Baroque, separated from the street by a small garden. It has heavy bossed pilasters, as well as Dutch pilasters, and is decorated with sculptures by Matěj Jackel from 1691. The two altar paintings (*The Holy Family* and *St. Anna*) are by Petr Brandl.

69

The Tuscan Palace
1689-91
Jean Baptiste Mathey, Giacomo Antonio Canevalle
1: Hradčany, Hradčanské náměstí 5
streetcar 22: *Pohořelec* or *Brusnice*

An Early Baroque palace in Roman style, which develops around a rectangular courtyard, enclosing the whole western face of the square. The calm façade is divided by two "towers"; the lower parts have entrances with pillared portals, topped with balconies, carrying sculptured coats of arms. Above the attic, the towers rise as two roof-top pavilions with a mansard roof. They are connected by a balustrade with sculptures of antique gods.

70

The Church of St. Jacob with the Minorite Monastery
1232, rebuilt in 1689-1702, interior 1736-39
Jan Šimon Pánek (Panecyus)

1: Staré Město, Malá Štupartská
metro B: *Náměstí Republiky*

The monastery was founded in 1232; the adjacent church was built between 1319 and 1374. It was later reconstructed in the Baroque style after a fire. The long Gothic basilical area with the elongated presbytery was preserved and enhanced with Baroque galleries above the lateral naves. The walls are segmented by *faux marbre* pilasters and decorated with stuccos by A. Bolla. F. Voget's 1736 main vault fresco was repainted in 1881. The interior was provided with a number of altars and church furnishings. Noteworthy is the sepulchre of Jan Václav Vratislav of Mitrovice, designed by J.B. Fischer von Erlach, with statuary by F.M. Brokoff. The painting above the main altar is the work of V.V. Reiner, while the interior also contains paintings by Petr Brandl. The adjacent Minorite Monastery preserves its Gothic origins in the north and west wings; the other two were rebuilt in the Baroque style. A corridor connects the south wing with the Gothic sacristy at the end of the chancel.

71

The Riding Academy at the Prague Castle

ca. 1694

Jean-Baptiste Mathey, Giacomo Antonio Canevalle

1: Hradčany, U Prašného mostu 3-5

streetcar 22: Pražský hrad

The Early Baroque building of the Winter Riding Academy with high, originally blind arcades, and small oval windows close to the ceiling, is 90 meters long. It has a narrow street-side façade, rhythmicized by a high Tuscan order. In 1697 the perpendicular wing of the Summer Riding Academy with a two-story arcade was added. In 1947-49 both the Academies were reconstructed to serve as exhibition halls, designed by Pavel Janák.

72

Sternberg Palace

1698-1720

Domenico Martinelli, Giovanni Battista Alliprandi, Giovanni Santini

1: Hradčany, Hradčanské náměstí 15

streetcar 22: Pražský hrad

One of the most important Baroque palaces, accessible only through the walkway in the western buttress of the Archbishop's Palace. It is a four-winged building, laid out around an inner courtyard. A high cylindrical buttress with tall windows on the ground floor is developed into a small garden behind the palace. A monumental stairway decorated with plastics by M. Braun rises from the entrance vestibule at the corner of the palace. The rooms on the first floor contain ceiling paintings, probably by M.V. Halwachs, from 1707. The palace houses the National Gallery of Prague.

73

Church of St. Ursula
Marco Antonio Canevalle
1: Nové Město, Národní třída
metro B: *Národní*; streecar 5, 9, 18, 22: *Národní divadlo*

The church belongs to the ensemble of the Ursuline convent, and is built on a rather unique plan. Its main façade is oriented from the street side, i.e. laterally. Its wall is arched at the centre, (as an harbinger of the later dynamic Baroque), in the centre is the entrance leading directly into the hall space, which is outfitted with very ornate Baroque furnishings. On a side altar is a painting of *The Annunciation of the Virgin Mary*, by Petr Brandl.

74

Church of St. Nicholas
1704-11, 1737-52 and 1755
Christoph Dientzenhofer, Kilian Ignaz Dientzenhofer, Anselmo Lurago
1: Malá Strana, Malostranské náměstí
streetcar 12, 22: *Malostranské náměstí*

The church was built as part of a Jesuit college. In the first phase Christoph Dientzenhofer built in the spirit of radical High Baroque the dynamic western façade convexly and concavely arched, as well as the nave to the depth of two bays. The work was completed a quarter of a century later by K.I. Dientzenhofer, who had the third bay vaulted.

He also created a trifoliate termination of the nave, crowned with a cupola seated on a high tambour, and accompanied by an high slim belltower, 74 meters high. The ceiling fresco in the vault of the main nave is the work of Jan L. Kracker; the authors of the frescos in the side aisles and the presbytery are František Xaver Palko, Josef Kramolín, and Josef Hager. The sculptural decoration is by Jan Bedřich Kohl, Ignaz Platzer, and the Prachner family.

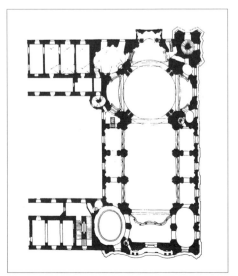

75

The Palace of the Hrzáns of Harasov
1702-10
Giovanni Battista Alliprandi
1: Staré Město, Celetná 12

metro A, B: Můstek

The palace was built on the remains of old Romanesque and Gothic houses. Its arrangement is attributable to Italian Mannerism, but it is naturally driven by the desire to create an illusion of movement, so characteristic of the High Baroque architecture. The architectural elements receive human form, aided by sculptors. This includes not just the bearing elements around the façade, but also the decorative parts. The palace was converted in to residences at the beginning of this century.

76

Lobkowitz Palace
1707 and 1769
Giovanni Battista Alliprandi, Ignaz Palliardi
1: Malá Strana, Vlašská 19

streetcar 12, 22: Malostranské náměstí

One of Prague's most important Baroque palaces. It has a symmetrical three-winged disposition, with the front tract courtyard vaulted by a cylindrical buttress. The latter is penetrated in the lower part by an arcade. The lateral wings are curved in the plan, in keeping with the closed Baroque curvature of the courtyard. The façade on the street is monumental, yet restrained, with a massive portal and a triangular gable in a mansard roof. Another floor was added to the palace in the middle of the 18th century. Earlier in the century one of the largest Baroque gardens was established on the site of a vineyard behind the palace. The entrance is through a barred gate, set on pillars decorated with sandstone statuary. In 1870 the garden was converted into an English park containing the first rock garden in Bohemia.

72

77
Kaiserstein Palace
after 1700
Giovanni Battista Alliprandi
1: Malá Strana, Malostranské náměstí 23
streetcar 12, 22: *Malostranské náměstí*

A High Baroque palace, serially structured, has three stories with an arcaded ground floor, bossed lateral chords, very wide suprafenestration, forming a highly decorated band. The window sills are corrugated and decorated with floral festoons. The palace is completed by a cornice, carried on doubled and tripled voluted consoles, above which there is a full straight attic with reliefs of the four seasons. At the end of the 19th century a balcony was placed on the façade.

78
The Benedictine Monastery with the Church of St. Margaret at Břevnov
1708-21 and 1745
Christoph Dientzenhofer, Kilian Ignaz Dientzenhofer
6: Břevnov, Markétská ulice
streetcar 8, 22: *Břevnovský klášter*

The monastery was built on the site of the original medieval convent, destroyed during the Hussite Wars. It constitutes a large precinct, which is entered through a decorative gate, built into an ensemble of domestic buildings. An alley leads to the main entrance of the church, to

which are connected at the rear the actual monastic buildings, developed around three inner courtyards. In the eastern tract are the accessible areas of the convent: on the first floor a gallery decorated by frescos depicting events from the history of the convent, while in the adjoining prelature there is a receiving salon decorated with wall paintings of idealized landscapes. The principal space of the prelature is the so-called Theresian Hall with rich ceiling stuccos, and an important ceiling fresco by K.D. Asam from 1727, considered to be the most valuable and best preserved Baroque fresco in Prague. Dominating the precinct is the Church of St. Margaret, a superior work in the style of Illusionistic Baroque, with a single-aisle disposition and undulated walls, which create a most affective space. Discovered under the church was a three-sided crypt, generously decorated with Pre-Romanesque pilasters. In the rear part of the convent garden is a small pavilion with the natural water spring Vojtěška; the delicate, distinctly modelled building is by Kilian Ignaz Dientzenhofer.

79
Zbraslav Chateau (Cistercian Convent Aula Regia)
1292 and 1709-39
Giovanni Santini, František Maxmilián Kaňka
5: Zbraslav, U Národní galerie
bus 129, 165, 241, 243, 245, 255: *Zbraslavské náměstí*

Originally a Cistercian convent and the burial place of Czech kings, it was first destroyed during the Hussite Wars, and again during the Thirty Years' War. Today the ensemble of the convent, chateau, and brewery lies in a large garden. The convent is a High Baroque three-wing building with an entrance courtyard, and a hallway leading through the whole building. Attached to the latter on the north side is a refectory, decorated with elaborate Rococo stucco. The central wing, oriented towards a terrace above the river, houses on the upper floor the Royal Hall, decorated with a fresco by V.V. Reiner. In front of the convent is the originally Gothic Church of St. Jacob, later adapted in the Early Baroque style.

On the north side is the former prela-

cy, now the Chateau, rebuilt by F.M. Kaňka and then redesigned in 1911-12 by D. Jurkovič. On the first floor are halls with frescos depicting events from the history of the convent.

80
Church of the Holiest Trinity
1712
Ottavio Broggio
1: Nové Město, Spálená ulice
metro B: *Národní*; streetcar 3, 9, 14, 24: *Lazarská*

The church was built as part of the no longer extant Trinitarian monastery. It is a three-aisled open hall with a cupola above the nave, and a square presbytery. A quiet façade is distinctly divided into three fields, with three large windows and three portals, crowned by a voluted gable. The Cubist arcade by A. Pfeiffer from 1913, which conceals M.J. Brokoff's statue of St. John Nepomuciensis, connects the church with the Cubist "Diamant" house next door.

81

Clam-Gallas Palace
1713-19
Johann Bernhard Fischer von Erlach
1: Staré Město, Husova 20
metro A; streetcar 17, 18: *Staroměstská*
Built in place of an earlier Gothic estate, it

was intended to announce the grandiose reconstruction of this part of the Old Town. This is why its monumental, richly plastically segmented façade is not designed to face a narrow street, but rather an open expanse; this, however, was never achieved. The main façade is divided by three buttresses. The side buttresses are penetrated by portals, decorated with titans by M. Braun, and terminated by a balustraded attic, topped at one time with 13 statues of classical gods. A multi-winged building of an irregular plan embraces two inner courtyards. The main edifice contains large halls, including a theatre, which are reached by an elaborately resolved palace stairway, decorated with light standards and vases by M. Braun. A ceiling fresco is by C. Carlone, who also decorated some of the rooms, and the library. It is one of Fischer's most important buildings, unique in the ensemble of Prague's Baroque heritage.

82

The Morzine Palace
1713-14
Giovanni Santini
1: Malá Strana, Nerudova 5
streetcar 12, 22: *Malostranské náměstí*
One of Prague's most important Baroque buildings and an example of the dynamic approach, characteristic for Santini. The ground floor of the palace is undulated and penetrated by two massively developed portals, one of which is blind. Placed on top of the portals are an allegorical "Sun and Night", spaning them is a balcony, supported by two Moorish figures by Ferdinand Maximilián Brokoff. Above the tall window of the middle buttress is a raised emblem of the family. The attic is crowned with statues of four continents.

83
Thun Palace
1716-27
Giovanni Battista Alliprandi, Jan Antonín Lurago
1: Malá Strana, Thunovská 14
streetcar 12, 22: Malostranské náměstí
A Neo-Gothic gate from 1850 opens onto a courtyard of a spacious palace, created through reconstruction and addition to the older Leslie House. Dominating the ensemble is a polygonal tower in the old core. Under the slope of the Prague Castle behind the palace is a landscaped garden.

84
Summer Palace of Jan Václav Michna of Vacínov (Villa Amerika)
1717-20
Kilian Ignaz Dientzenhofer
2: Nové Město, ulice Ke Karlovu 20
metro C; streetcar 4, 16, 22: I.P. Pavlova
The first independent building of Kilian Ignaz in Prague. A small summer residence with a mansard roof and a plastically segmented façade, whose rich decoration evokes a Hildebrandian inspiration from the architect's journeyman travels. However, here they already carry the author's own motifs: the concave pilasters of the middle buttress as well as the roof dormers with volute wings.

The villa stands in a symmetrically segmented garden, with the entrance to the chamber area flanked by two pavilions. The totality, inclusive of the sculptural decorations, creates, even on this small scale, a singularly balanced composition.

85
Church of St. John Nepomuciensis
1720-29
Kilian Ignaz Dientzenhofer
1: Hradčany, Kanovnická ulice
streetcar 22: Brusnice

It is the earliest ecclesiastical building of Dientzenhofer. Its floor plan is in the shape of a Greek cross, with an octagonal main space, vaulted by a Bohemian flat vault. The adjacent area of chapels and a sacristy has a right-angle plan. Above the façade with a Viennese-style portal is a tower aligned with them. The vault of the central nave is decorated with a fresco by V.V. Reiner. Adjacent to the church is the building of the former Ursuline convent, built after 1721.

86
The Thun-Hohenstein Palace
1720-25
Giovanni Santini
1: Malá Strana, Nerudova 20
streetcar 12, 22: Malostranské náměstí

The latest wing of a large compound, built by Santini on the site of five Lesser Side houses. The symmetrical façade, with the ground floor rising evenly with the level of the street, is dominated by the central portico, extended slightly above the attic. On its ground floor it has a monumental entrance bordered by heraldic eagles, above the carriage entrance, on a dynamically corrugated sill, are figures of Juno and Jupiter by Matthias Braun. The portal is accompanied on both sides by low vaulted entrances, with oval windows above them. The pillared entrance vestibule is decorated with Braun's statues. The stairway from the vestibule was designed by J. Zítek, and built at the end of the 19th century. The posterior oldest part of the palace reaches all the way to the Castle Steps. It is a Renaissance building with characteristic gables and a façade decorated with diamond-point graffito.

87

The Písek Gate (also known as Bruská)
1721
Christoph Dientzenhofer
6: Hradčany, U písecké brány 20
metro A: *Hradčanská*

Built as part of Prague's new fortifications after the Thirty Years' War, it is a very massive building with bossed corners, a narrow steeply vaulted carriage way, two small pedestrian gates, and an earth-covered roof. The carved military emblems are by Jan Oldřich Mayer. This was the terminal since 1828 of the first horse-drawn railway to Lány, and from 1843, of the steam-powered railway to Olomouc and Dresden.

88

Church of St. Gallus
before 1232 and 1722-29
Giovanni Santini (?)
1: Staré Město, Havelská ulice
metro A, B: *Můstek*

Once a convent church of the Carmelites, it was rebuilt in the 14th century into a High Gothic basilica with a long chancel. At the beginning of the 18th century a rippled wall in the style of Illusionistic Baroque was built in front of the façade.

Above the façade were statues of Carmelite saints and of John Nepomuciensis. The interior of the church presents an appealing combination of Gothic and Baroque. The Gothic ribbed vaults are preserved, at he end of the chancel there are uneven masonry arcades, on the sides Early Baroque galleries, and at the end of the side naves are Baroque chapels.

89

Faust's House

2nd half of the 16th century and 1725
František Maxmilián Kaňka, Antonín Karel
Schmidt (?)
2: Nové Město, Karlovo náměstí 40
metro B: Karlovo náměstí; streetcar 3, 4, 14, 16, 18, 22, 24:
Karlovo náměstí or Moráň

Essentially a Gothic house, later adapted in the Renaissance style with joined windows and a distinctive corner oriel. It was rebuilt twice during the Baroque period.
The central buttress has a high decorative gable and an opulent arrangement above the windows. The western portal is the work of Kilian Ignaz Dientzenhofer.

90

The Portheimka Villa

1725
Kilian Ignaz Dientzenhofer
5: Smíchov, Štefánikova ulice 12
metro B; streetcar 4, 6, 7, 9, 12, 14, 16: Anděl

The architect's private suburban villa has a rectangular plan with four corner observation pavilions, to which are adjoined lateral bi-planar wings. On the ground floor a sala terrena opened into the garden. Above it was a stately hall with a domical vault, decorated with a fresco by Václav Vavřinec Reiner. In the first third of the 19th century the wings were enlarged and rebuilt in the Classicist style. The southern wing was demolished in 1881.

91

Church of St. Bartholomew

1726-31
Kilian Ignaz Dientzenhofer
1: Staré Město, Bartolomějská ulice
metro B; streetcar 9, 18, 22: Národní třída

The church was built as part of a Jesuit convent. Its irregular ground plan points towards the use of masonry from an older building. The entrance hall and the presbytery are broadly interconnected with the hall of the central nave. The vaulting is decorated with frescos of V.V. Reiner. To the street the church presents a very modest façade. However to the convent's inner yard it displays a decorative wall with large vestment-shaped windows.

92
Church of St. Thomas
1285-1316, 1551, 1584 and 1727-31
baroque reconstruction by *Kilian Ignaz*
Dientzenhofer

1: Malá Strana, Letenská ulice

streetcar 12, 22: *Malostranské náměstí*

The convent church was built as a triple-aisled basilica of the mendicant type. It was one of the most opulent churches in Prague. After suffering static damage, it was rebuilt in the first third of the 18th century, when it received elaborate Baroque architectural articulation. The original barrel vaulting was replaced by flat vaults tied into jack arches. In the first bay of the presbytery a low cupola was raised. The main façade, addressing a narrow street. was rebuilt in the style of Illusionistic Baroque. The broken pediment responds to both close views, and panoramic distant views.

Preserved was the Late Renaissance façade by G. Bossi, the statue of St. Augustin by J. Kohl, as well as the statue of St. Thomas above the side portal. The ceiling paintings inside are by V.V. Reiner from 1728-30. The main altar is decorated by copies of paintings by P.P. Rubens, while the side altars have works of B. Spranger, K. Škréta, and F.X. Balko.

93

Church of St. Nicholas

1732-35
Kilian Ignaz Dientzenhofer
1: Staré Město, Staroměstské náměstí
metro A: *Staroměstská*

Built as part of a Benedictine monastery, no longer extant. Originally the church was part of the square, separated from it by the Kren house. It was situated towards the narrow street behind the City Hall, to which it offered the main façade with a high central cupola and two slim towers on the southern side. Dispositionally it is an extended central nave on a cruciform plan, with a deep chamber under the choir and a semicircularly terminated presbytery. The sculptural decoration of the façade is by Antonín Braun, the fresco in the cupola by Kosmas D. Asam.

94

Invalidovna

1729-37
Kilian Ignaz Dientzenhofer
8: Karlín, Sokolovská ulice 136
metro B: *Invalidovna*

Originally intended as an extensive charitable institution for military invalids and their families. A square, with a side of 300 meters, was to be divided into nine courtyards, with the central one accomodating a church. For financial reasons only one of the courtyards was completed. It is surrounded by a covered two-story gallery, from which the individual living quarters can be reached. The latter are resolved in two planes. The architecture is somewhat baroquely Classicist, austere and modest, using only shallow buttresses, topped with gables and attics. These are crowned with sculptural decorations.

95

Church of St. John Nepomuciensis at the Rock (U Skalka)

1730-38
Kilian Ignaz Dientzenhofer
2: Nové Město, Vyšehradská ulice

metro B: Karlovo náměstí; streetcar 3, 4, 14, 16, 18, 24: Moráň

Built on the site of a 17th century chapel, it is an octagonal central space with concavely involuted walls, a transversly situated oval vestibule between two slanted towers, and a presbytery of the same ground plan. All the spaces are vaulted with Bohemian flat vaults. The fresco *Celebration of St. John Nepomuciensis* is the work of Karel Kovář, while the wooden altar sculpture of the same saint is by Jan Brokoff.

96

Church of St. Charles Borromeo (now of St. Cyril and St. Methodius)

1735-40
Kilian Ignaz Dientzenhofer
2: Nové Město, Resslova ulice

metro B; streetcar 3, 4, 6, 14, 16, 22, 24: Karlovo náměstí

The unusually situated church at the corner of a block of houses once belonged to a former home for elderly clergymen, to which it was attached. It consists of a single-hall space with three vaulted bays, a presbytery, and an anteroom; the northern side is bordered by a gallery. It is decorated with frescos by K. Schopf, lined by stuccos of I. Palliardi. The entrance is through a courtyard, which, following an end of the 18th century renovation, ended up on a raised terrace. The church is accented by a tower, raised directly in the axis of the façade. Under the church lies a crypt.

97

House at the Cats (U Kočků)
present appearance 1736
1: Staré Město, Karlova 44

metro A: Staroměstská

One of the first impressive Romanesque houses in Prague – the Romanesque part is preserved in the basement – rebuilt later in the Gothic style, as evident from the ground floor vaults. It was rebuilt again during the Renaissance. The current mode is Baroque, designed by Bartolomeo Scotti, with an interior stairway decorated with I. Platzer's sculptures. The walkway was added in the 20th century.

98

Colloredo-Mansfeld Palace
1735-47
František Ignác Prée
1: Staré Město, Karlova 2

metro A; streetcar 17, 18: Staroměstská

Created in the Old Town, it replaced several Early Gothic houses. The building envelopes two inner courtyards and has a relatively flat façade, accentuated in the middle section by an elaborate portal decorated by Matthias Braun. Significant is the main hall in the court tract, an eliptical plan fitted into a rectangular space, which allows for arcades and galleries in the corners. The vault of the hall is decorated by Giovanni Pietro Scotti's fresco.

99

Church of St. Catherine
1737-41
Kilian Ignaz Dientzenhofer

streetcar 18, 24: Botanická zahrada

The church is a hall-like edifice with a central transept, covered with Bohemian flat vaulting. Václav Vavřinec Reiner's grandiose ceiling paintings in individual fields are enhanced by elaborate stucco decoration of B. Spinetti. The slender octagonal tower, divided into several floors, remains from an older Gothic church (dated before 1367). The church belonged to the Augustian monastery which was closed in 1787.

100

Sylva-Taroucca (Piccolomini) Palace
1744-1752
Kilian Ignaz Dientzenhofer, Anselmo Lurago
1: Nové Město, Na Příkopě 10
metro A, B: Můstek

The palace was on a deep and narrow Gothic lot, developed around three inner courtyards. Exceptional is the main façade with heavily bossed dual pillars around the carriage and passage ways. It has a distinctively raised first floor, and a low loft under a segmented roof attic with a number of historicizing Early Baroque elements. The first tract contains a vestibule, connected to a Rococo stairway, decorated with plastics by I.F. Platzer, stuccos by C.G. Bossi, and a fresco by V. Ambrož. In the third tract there is a small pillar hall, adapted in the Baroque style in 1878.

101

Church of St. Michael
1313 and 1750
František Ignác Prée
1: Staré Město,
Melantrichova 17
metro A, B: Můstek

Originally a Gothic five-aisle church with a quadrangular tower. After 1620 it was given to the Servites, who rebuilt it in the Baroque style, added an entrance hall with a beautiful Bohemian vault, and built a monastery, replacing several town houses.
The church was decorated with frescos and opulent altars.
At the end of the 18th century both church and monastery were closed and their furnishings were moved to churches in Líbeznice, Rokycany, and Sokolov.

102

Golz-Kinský Palace
1755-65
Kilian Ignaz Dientzenhofer, Anselmo Lurago
1: Staré Město, Staroměstské náměstí 12
metro A: *Staroměstská*
The building enters into the area at the eastern wall of the square, on the site of a Gothic house, later rebuilt in the Renaissance style.

The Late Baroque building already has Rococo stuccos on the façade. The attic is decorated with sculptures of the elements by I. Platzer. The separate tracts of the palace have differently conceived staircases. The first tract includes a succession of connected halls, adapted in 1835 by the architect J. Koch. Attached to the palace on the north side is a recessed house, which has a façade in the Neo-Rococo style.

103

Kolowrat Palace
ca. 1780
Ignaz Palliardi
1: Malá Strana, Valdštejnská 10
metro A: *Malostranská*; streetcar 12, 22: *Malostranské náměstí*

One of the last of Prague's Baroque palaces, its façade gently follows the curve of the street. It is divided by a central shallow buttress, accentuated by pilasters and a gable.

At the rear of the palace is the small building, known as the Little Černín Palace, built in 1770. Adjacent is the entrance to the terrace of a Rococo garden, built in 1769-89, and decorated with several gazebos, a stairway, and ballustrades. It culminates in a three-part sala terrena above which stands an oval-shaped garden cottage. The interior of the palace was rebuilt in the mid-19th century.

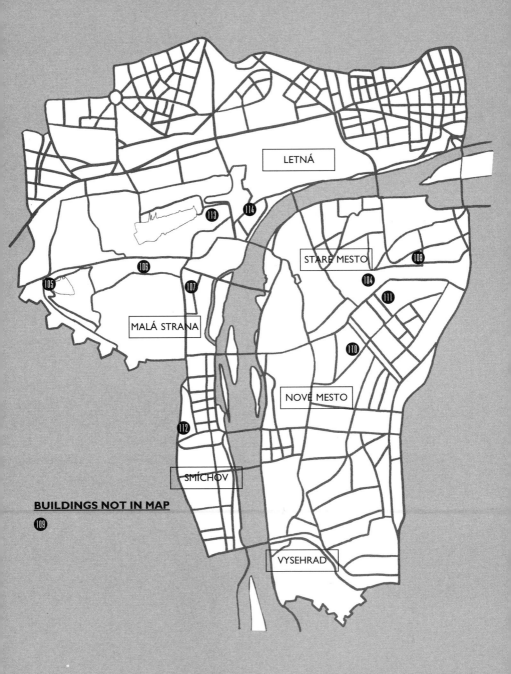

LETNÁ

STARÉ MESTO

MALÁ STRANA

NOVE MESTO

SMÍCHOV

VYSEHRAD

BUILDINGS NOT IN MAP

109

Classicist Prague

The social situation of Prague changed from the end of the 18th century. The city definitely lost its character as the royal seat, and the middle classes gradually replaced the aristocracy in importance. The reforms introduced by Josef II, which led to the closure of a large number of churches and convents, reduced the importance of the Church. The highly dynamic architecture no longer suited the character of life in Prague, which grew more civilian and quotidian. Inspiration by pure antiquity appeared, but it was not applied too frequently: the oncoming rationalism did not contain within it the need for prestigious display. Karlín, a purely bourgeois new residential district, was established in Prague. The first tenement buildings appeared in streets and along the embankment, as well as new types of buildings, such as hospitals, theatres, military barracks, and administrative buildings. Public parks were also being established. However, outstanding buildings in the Classicist style are rare.

104

The Estates' Theatre
1781-83
Antonín Haffenecker
1: Staré Město, Železná ulice 11
metro A, B: Můstek

One of the first buildings in Bohemia influenced by the Classicist style, it was built on a long rectangular plan of a picture-frame type theatre. All the exterior façades were symmetrical, with central buttresses, enclosed by triangular gables. The buttress in the main façade is lined by four Corinthian columns above the carriage underpass. In the soft curvature of the façade the last resonances of the Baroque can still be felt. The theatre was rebuilt in the mid-19th century, receiving new entrances and staircases, including a separate staircase to the royal box on the south side. The iron balconies on the first floor are from this same period.

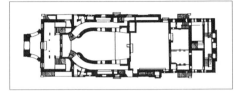

105

The Library of the Strahov Monastery
1782-84
Ignaz Palliardi
1: Hradčany, Strahovské nádvoří
streetcar 22: Pohořelec

The Hall of Philosophy consists of a whole building with a distinctive façade, which documents the transition from the Baroque feeling towards Classicism. The high façade is calm, divided into three fields by high pilasters with Tuscan capitals. It has characteristic motifs of garlands, rosettes and triglyphs in the frieze under the sectioned gable, decorated by typical vases in the Louis Seize style. Inside, the hall encompasses both floors. The walls are lined with richly decorated bookcases, separated at two thirds of their height by a gallery. The vault is decorated by Antonín Maulbertsch's fresco *The History of Mankind*. The library has a collection of rare manuscripts. The Library has a collection of rare manuscripts.

106
Lichtenstein Palace (Ledeburg)
façade: 1791
Matěj Hummel

1: Malá Strana, Malostranské náměstí 13

streetcar 12, 22: Malostranské náměstí

Originally an ensemble of five Gothic town houses, gradually unified into a single residence, rebuilt during the Renaissance. While the exterior façade is unified by Classicist adaptation, the diversity of the original composition is still apparent. The palace has a shallow buttress with an entrance portal and a wide, low-slung vaulting, decorated with Classicist vases. The courtyard tract, created from a Renaissance urban villa, contains a large hall. The palace, including the interiors, was ultimately unified during the reconstruction of 1993, designed by P. Kupka.

107
Rohan Palace
1796, 1807 and 1838
Josef Klement Zobel, Louis Montoyer, Vincenc Kulhánek
1: Malá Strana, Karmelitská 8

streetcar 12, 22: Malostranské náměstí

The original palace underwent an early 19th century stately reconstruction for the Duchess Kuronská. A refined ballroom in the style of the hall at Vienna's Hofburg, with columns and opulent decoration belongs to that period. Subsequently the façade was rebuilt in a restrained Classicist style, with a bossed ground floor and Corinthian pilasters of the central portico, completed by a trapezoidal gable.

108
Palace U Hybernů
1808-11
Jiří Fischer
1: Nové Město, Náměstí Republiky 3

metro B; streetcar 5, 14, 26: Náměstí Republiky

Originally a Baroque convent church (1652-59), which was closed and consequently rebuilt as a Customs House. The former church was turned into a customs warehouse, with a monumental symmetrical façade inspired by the style of the Berlin mint. In the 20th century it was rebuilt into an exhibition hall.

109

The Borough of Karlín
1817
8: Karlín, Křižíkova, Thámova, Pobřežní,
Těšnov

metro B; streetcar 8, 24: *Křižíkova*

The first Prague suburb outside of the Poříč Gate
had a regulatory plan determined by decree,
based on the ideas of enlightened urban development, tested during the construction of gar-
rison residences. For this reason, its streets are
wide and laid out on a grid; it also has a
block-wide landscaped town square. The mostly three-story tenement houses were built in the
spirit of Classicism.

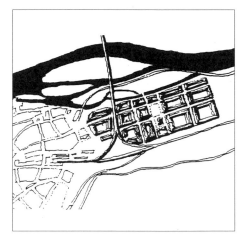

110

Platýz House
1813-47
Jindřich Hausknecht
1: Staré Město, Národní třída

metro B: *Národní třída* or *Můstek*

The first Prague rental house, built on the site of
a Renaissance building, has an elongated façade
with three wide buttresses, with a very flat
plasticity of simple cornices. Only the buttresses above the first floor window have triangular
frontons. The ground floor is segmented by
arched display windows. The passageway into a
courtyard is located in the centre between them.
The top of the house is terminated in the buttress by a triangular gable above a cornice.

111

Church of the Holy Cross
1819-24
Jiří Fischer
1: Nové Město, Na Příkopě 19

metro A, B: *Můstek*

The first sacral Classicist building, built in conjunction with the Piarist Convent. The single-
naved hall is spanned by four flat vaults, while
the vaulted choir is separated by a triumphal arch
on doubled columns. The exterior appearance is
restrained and inspired by Prussian influences. The
entrance niche is lined by two Ionian columns,
with two pilasters linked to them. The building
is heavily enclosed above by a breastsummer, a
cornice, and an attic under the hip roof.

112
Kinský Summer Palace
1827-31
Jindřich Koch
5: Petřínské sady
streetcar 5, 9, 12: Petřínské sady

One of the few examples of a Classicist small chateau in a newly established English park. It stands on a divide, levelled by a terrace; this accounts for its two stories on the eastern side, with a portico carried by Doric columns, and a spacious balcony above, accessible from the main hall. The latter is columnar, vaulted by a cupola, illuminated from above. On the western side the chateau is only single-storied, with a massive carriage portico, carried on Ionian columns.

113
Klár's Institute for the Blind (presently Office of the Presidium of the Government)
1836-44
Vincenc Kulhánek, Josef Kranner
1: Malá Strana, Klárov 3
metro A; streetcar 12, 18, 22: Malostranská

A long building of a strict and austere nature, divided in the middle by a wide shallow buttress, which is terminated by a low triangular gable, with a relief by Josef Max. A slim tower with a high peak rises above the roof. Built later in the garden is the Chapel of St. Raphael with frescos in the Nazarene style.

114
Public Baths
1840
Josef Kanner
1: Malá Strana, Nábřeží Edvarda Beneše
metro A: Malostranská; streetcar 12, 17: Čechův most

The first public baths on the Vltava river included a small pavilion, whose central part opens through a portico with Doric columns and a triangular gable. Attached on the sides are lower and more modestly designed wings of the changing cabins, arranged around a top-lit cambered central corridor.

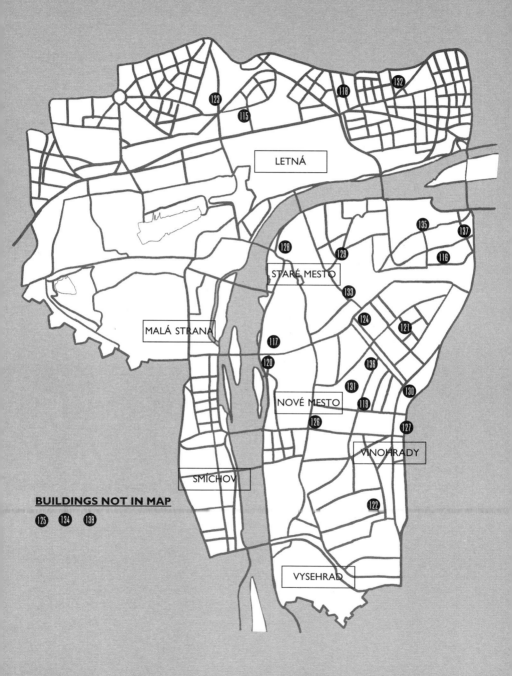

LETNÁ

STARÉ MESTO

MALÁ STRANA

NOVÉ MESTO

VINOHRADY

SMÍCHOV

VYSEHRAD

BUILDINGS NOT IN MAP

Architecture of the 19th Century

In the first third of the 19th century the Classicist style still ruled, but soon it could not keep up with the new needs of the aggressively developing city. The new bourgeoisie wanted to demonstrate its growing importance by erecting new buildings: it did not want to fall behind the old aristocratic largesse. It sought inspiration in ancient styles and put into place their contemporary forms. It was peculiar, however, that contemporary modifications of the highest styles did not really make their mark. The Neo-Gothic style dominated the infrequent new religious buildings, and by its careful emphasis on historical verisimilitude its expression became boring; the Neo-Baroque was altogether rare in Prague. It was mostly the Neo-Renaissance that overwhelmed the city, excellent particularly in the buildings of Ignác Ullmann, Josef Zítek, and Josef Schulz. The city modernized rapidly after the demolition of the medieval fortifications in 1871. Very quickly it grew into the adjacent municipalities such as Žižkov, Královské Vinohrady, Smíchov and others. New types of buildings appeared, especially financial institutions, schools, hotels, museums, and a variety of office buildings. Besides these, the first urban villas and tenement houses were being built in the Neo-Renaissance style based on Italian traditions. These were seen as a sign of progressivness. The building of the National Theatre gave the Neo-Renaissance a distinctly nationalistic focus.

115

The Viceregal Summer Palace at Stromovka
1811
Jiří Fischer
7: Bubeneč, Královská obora
bus 131: *Sibiřské náměstí*

Originally a hunting chateau from the end of the 15th century, rebuilt during the Renaissance. The reconstruction of the viceregal summer palace presents a very early example of the romanti-

cizing Neo-Gothic style. Following the example of the Franzenburg Chateau at the Luxemburg Park in Vienna, and inspired also by English Neo-Gothicism.

Fischer particularly redesigned the exterior appearance. The large arcades were pointed, in some places doubled, and filled with glazed wooden rounded ribbing. On the interfenestral pillars gothicizing vertical supports were created to carry the lunette cornice. Above is a richly decorated attic.

116

Desfour Palace
1846
Josef Kranner
1: Nové Město, Na Florenci 21
metro B, C: *Florenc*

Externally a rather ordinary Neo-Renaissance palace within the regular streetscape, it excels especially in its interiors, richly decorated in the style of the Second Rococo. An elegant staircase leads up to the first floor halls, which are decorated by numerous wall paintings. The grand ballroom contains important glass-work with figures from period operas. A garden composed in the French style used to be connected to the palace.

117
Czech Academy of Sciences
1861 and 1894-96
Ignác Ullmann, František Šachner
1: Staré Město, Národní třída 5
streetcar 9, 18, 22: *Národní divadlo*

The Neo-Renaissance palace was built originally as the home of the Czech Savings Bank, with a monumental, though plastically unimpressive façade, and a spacious entrance vestibule above the staircase. The left side was added later to match the original project.

118
Restaurant "Letenský zámeček"
1861-63
Ignác Ullmann
7: Holešovice, Letenské sady (Kostelní 7)
streetcar 1, 8, 25, 26: *Letenské náměstí*

The garden pavilion is built in the style of an Italian Renaissance villa, with an asymmetrically seated tower. It has an accentuated central buttress, which is segmented by arcade windows and pilasters with Corinthian capitals.

119
Finishing School for Girls
1867
Ignác Ullmann
1: Nové Město, Vodičkova 20
streetcar 3, 9, 14, 24: *Vodičkova*

An important example of a Czech Neo-Renaissance building, severely symmetrical, with a massive central buttress, and a distinctive plastic cornice, set high. The whole edifice is elaborately segmented by massive bossages, and decorated above the windows with figurative and ornamental graffito.

120
The National Theatre
1868-83
Josef Zítek, Josef Schulz
1: Nové Město, Národní třída
streetcar 9, 17, 18, 22: *Národní divadlo*
One of the most beautiful examples of 19th century Prague architecture. Inspired stylistically by the Italian Late Renaissance, it was built on the site of an old salt-house. On the south side

it is tied into the small Temporary Theatre (Prozatimní divadlo), which was by I. Ullmann. It occupies an irregular trapezoidal lot. Above the entrance portal, a high columnar loggia topped by a balustrade with statues of the Muses opens above an advanced heavy portico. Massive corner pylons are terminated by ceremonial trigae. The rich interior decoration is the work of the group of artists, known as the generation of the National Theatre.

121
Schebek's Palace
1869-71
Ignác Ullmann
1: Nové Město, Politických vězňů 7
metro A, B: Můstek; A, C: *Muzeum*
One of Prague's most important Neo-Renaissance residential buildings with a massive entrance portico, a spacious inner courtyard, and a luxurious columned vestibule. On the upper floors there are preserved ceiling paintings on the vaults of the hallways.

122

The State Maternity Hospital
1867-75
Josef Hlávka
2: Nové Město, Apolinářská 18
metro C: I.P. Pavlova

Externally the building is conceived in the style of brick Neo-Gothic with elements of stone and details decorated by black and green glazing. It is a very modern construction in terms of layout – six parallel pavilions are connected by corridors, with all the rooms facing south, with adjacent birthing and operating rooms. On the north end the ensemble is connected to an administration building and a chapel; the south end houses the technical support facilities.

123

Lanna's Villa
1870
Ignác Ullmann
6: Bubeneč, V sadech 24
metro A: Hradčanská

One of the first examples of a prestigious modern urban villa. While it is modelled after Italian Renaissance villas, it is not merely an external imitation, but rather it considers local climatic conditions. The entrance is outlined by four slim columns of the portico, above which sits a spacious loggia. The inner areas, decorated with paintings, are concentrated around a hall with a palace stairway.

124

Haas's House
1871
Theophil Hansen
1: Nové Město, Na Příkopě 4
metro A, B: Můstek
One of the oldest department stores in Prague
with a cast iron structure, and a stone façade in
the style of Italian Late Renaissance. It has an unusual stairway on the inside.

125

Groebe's Villa
1871-88
Antonín Barvitius, Josef Schulz
2: Vinohrady, Havlíčkovy sady
streetcar 4, 22: Krymská
A summer home built in the style of Italian Renaissance in the middle of a designed garden,
with rich architectural decoration – a man-
made cave, cascades, hothouses, a fountain, a
gazebo – all are directly tied into a vineyard. The
two story villa excels through its monumental
entrance portico and rich Neo-Renaissance interior decoration.

126

The Czech Technical University
1872-74
Ignác Ullmann
2: Nové Město, Karlovo náměstí
metro B; streetcar 3, 4, 14, 16, 18, 22, 24: Karlovo náměstí
A massive edifice built according to the winning
competition design in the style of Italian High
Renaissance, prominently segmented, with a
massive central buttress. In the deep niches
between entrances are statues of Labour and Sci-
ence. A circular palace stairway, supported by
Tuscan pillars, rises from the entrance hall.

127
The House of the Sculptor Bohuslav Schnirch
1875
Antonín Wiehl, Josef Zeyer, Jan Martin
2: Nové Město, Mikovcova 5
metro C: I.P. Pavlova

One of the most significant buildings of Czech Historicism, it is a dwelling with a sculptor's studio, built in pure Neo-Renaissance style with very delicate reliefs decorated by graffito friezes. The vestibule has a fountain with a statue of Mercury.

128
Rudolfinum
1876-84
Josef Zítek, Josef Schulz
1: Josefov, Náměstí Jana Palacha
metro A; streetcar 17, 18: *Staroměstská*

One of the most important Neo-Renaissance buildings in Prague is divided into two parts: a concert hall and an exhibition space. The two parts are distinctively differentiated on the outside by deep niches and also by different architectural grammar. The concert space is oriented into a town square. The extremely arched façade rises above a broad ceremonial stairway; the vault of the main hall which is flanked by promenades with salons, is carried on 18 tall Corinthian columns. The exhibition gallery is accessible from the embankment; its exhibition spaces are developed around a central hall with overhead lighting. A glazed loggia inspired by Raphael's "Stanzas" opens onto the embankment.

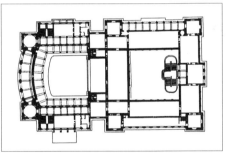

129
The Builders' Association Building
1875-79
Josef Schulz, Antonín Wiehl, Jan Zeyer
1: Staré Město, Kozí 7
metro A: *Staroměstská*
A refined Neo-Renaissance building, decorated with a wealth of paintings, frescos, and graffiti. Medallions between windows contain busts of important Czech builders and architects.

130
The National Museum
1885-90
Josef Schulz
1: Nové Město, Václavské náměstí
metro A, C: *Muzeum*
A monumental Neo-Renaissance building with a high cupola completes visually Wenceslas Square (Václavské náměstí). Its scale marks the modern largesse of this central city boulevard. The museum sits on a high landing with two access ramps and a trifurcate staircase. It has a distinctly protruding monumental central buttress, and is terminated at the corners by towers with low cupolas. On the inside the exhibition halls evolve along the whole circumference, while the interior space has a ceremonial hexabrachial staircase with arcade galleries.

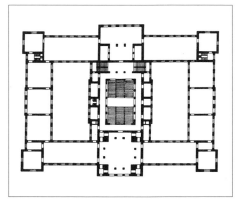

100

131
Hlávka's Tenements
1889
Josef Fanta
1: Nové Město, Vodičkova 15-17
streetcar 3, 9, 14, 24: *Vodičkova*

An ensemble of Neo-Renaissance tenement houses, covering the full depth of a block between two streets, outlining two inner courtyards. The houses have two tracts, resolved in such a way, that all the rooms receive direct daylight. On the ground floor are restaurants and shops with uniform portals. The façades are richly decorated with graffitos; notable is the Neo-Renaissance decoration of the walkways.

132
The Industrial Palace
1891
Bedřich Munzberger
7: Holešovice, Výstaviště
streetcar 5, 12, 17: *Výstaviště*

The palace was built on the occasion of the Jubilee Exhibition of the Kingdom of Bohemia. It has a steel frame and is divided into two long wings, attached to a central transverse aisle, delineated on the outside by massive corner pylons, with its center accentuated by a slim tower.

Reliefs of geniuses decorate the façade, while the side wings have busts of Czech engineers. The palace was rebuilt several times, its last adaptation having been done in the spirit of the so-called Socialist Realism in the 1950s.

133
The Municipal Savings Bank
1892-94
Antonín Wiehl, Osvald Polívka
1: Staré Město, Rytířská 29
metro A, B: Můstek

The refined Neo-Renaissance building was erected on the site of former small shops. Built originally as a two-story building on a regular rectangular plan, its corners are emphasized by shallow buttress towers. In the centre of the building, on the first floor, is a high hall, glazed above, accesible by a ceremonial stairway. The exteriors and interiors are lavishly decorated, exclusively by Czech artists.

134
Church of St. Ludmila
1893
Josef Mocker
2: Vinohrady, Náměstí Míru
metro A; streetcar 4, 16, 22: Náměstí Míru

A Neo-Gothic brick basilica, built in the strictly calculated style of the North German Gothic cathedrals, with two towers flanking the façade and a transept. The tympanum of the main portal carries a relief by J.V. Myslbek; the interior has wall paintings and glass-work in the windows was designed, among others, by F. Ženíšek and A. Liebscher. The side altars are newer and already show the vocabulary of the Secession.

135
The Rectory at St. Peter's
1893-1894
Antonín Wiehl
1: Nové Město, Biskupská
metro B, C: Florenc

An important Neo-Renaissance building, richly decorated with graffitos of Czech patrons from cartoons of Calda Klouček. The ground-floor portico displays a rather Neo-Romanesque character. Above the second floor extends a lunette cornice, above which evolves a formally complex attic floor.

136
House of the Architect Antonín Wiehl
1895-96
Antonín Wiehl
1: Nové Město, Václavské náměstí 34
metro A, B: Můstek; streetcar 3, 9, 14, 24: *Václavské náměstí*

A four-story corner house, owned originally by one of the proponents of Czech Neo-Renaissance. On the side facing the square it is segmented on the first floor by three large arched windows; on the floor above is added a shallow balcony, with an adjacent oriel extending over two floors. The roof is crowned by a tower and the gables are lined with Neo-Renaissance elements. The façade is covered with historical and ethnographic motifs from cartoons by M. Aleš.

137
Museum of the Capital City of Prague
1896-98
Antonín Balšánek, Antonín Wiehl
8: Karlín, Švermovy sady
metro B, C: *Florenc*

The building marks the end of Neo-Renaissance and the arrival of the freer expression of the Secession. The two-story two-tract building has a prominently rising buttress turned towards the park, and a tympanum with elaborate plastic decoration. Thrust behind the monumental entrance hall is the main stairway, which is tribrachially circular, with top lighting. It is decorated by a wall painting of the panorama of Prague.

138
The Vinohrady Market Hall
1902
Antonín Turek
2: Vinohrady, Vinohradská 50
metro A: *Náměstí Míru*

The basilical building of steel construction is one of the well preserved examples of industrial architecture in Prague. Preserved in the basement is the original air conditioning mechanical room, which served the underground warehouse areas.

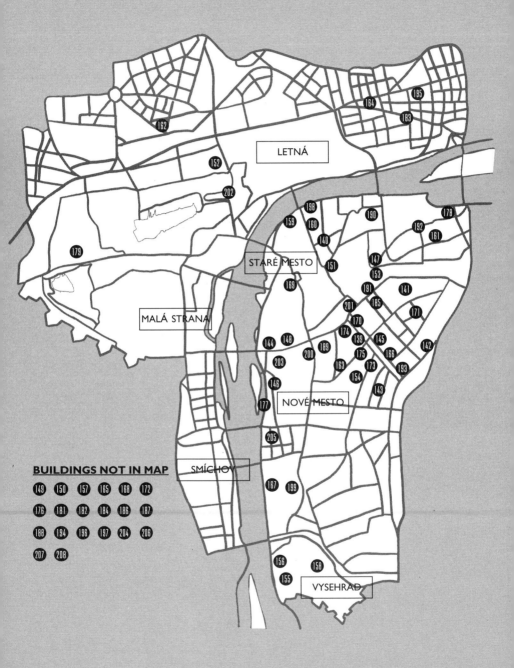

LETNÁ

STARÉ MESTO

MALÁ STRANA

NOVÉ MESTO

SMÍCHOV

VYSEHRAD

BUILDINGS NOT IN MAP

149 150 157 165 168 172

176 181 182 184 186 187

188 194 196 197 204 206

207 208

Architecture of the 20th Century

The building of the Exhibition Complex at the Jubilee Exhibition marked the arrival of the architecture of the Secession, which at the turn of the century became the style of the middle class. Soon, however, the curious new style of architectural Cubism was introduced in Prague. It was created by a small group of architects, including J. Chochol, J. Gočár, V. Hofman, P. Janák, and E. Králík, who, when independent Czechoslovakia was established, trade to make Cubism (also known as Rondocubism, or Small-Arch Cubism) into the official national style. Although some buildings were realized, it never really gained mass popularity.

Prague's architecture of the first half of the 20th century is marked by two approaches: the traditional, which makes frequent references to Classicism, and is used for official government buildings; and the modern, which culminated at the end of the 1920s in the excellent achievements of Functionalism. The latter became the leading movement, and was used on large administrative buildings, and on residential buildings. Functionalism is considered to be one of the finest trends in Czech architecture. The 1950s brought Socialist Realism to Prague. One of its intentions included a fundamental reconstruction of the historical core, and the creation of an enormous mass gathering area; in the end it contributed only two hotels – the International and the Jalta. In 1959 the development reconnected with the Functionalist experience, which corresponded with the rationalistic sensibility of the period. Most of the efforts were concentrated on large scale prefabricated housing projects. Even under these conditions, a few more distinctive buildings appeared, reacting to the contemporary European trands. Eventually, a new Functionalism evolved, resuming the celebrated traditions of the period between the wars.

139
Peterka's House
1899
Jan Koteřa
1: Nové Město, Václavské náměstí 12
metro A, B: Můstek

A Prague house with an Early Secession façade, cast iron elements on the window lintels and decorated with modest stucco and plastic decoration by S. Sucharda and J. Pekárek. The interior layout marks the principles of a modern utilitarian arrangement, with clear separation of the commercial ground floor and the living quarters.

140
Reclamation of the Jewish Quarter
ca. 1900
1: Josefov, Platnéřská, Kaprova, Pařížská, Široká
metro A: Staroměstská

The reclamation of the former ghetto was determined in 1885, principally for hygienic reasons. In 1889 a regulatory plan was approved, which substantially simplified the network of streets, straightened and widened them. It liquidated all edifices, with the exception of 6 synagogues, the cemetery, and the Town Hall. The building of new houses began at the start of the 20th century on the corner of Old Town Square and Pařížská Street. The new construction presents a richly varied ensemble of styles, from the historicizing and romantic, to the Secession.

|41|
Hotel Central

1899-1901
Friedrich Ohmann, Bedřich Bendelmayer, Alois Dryák
1: Nové Město, Hybernská 10
metro B: *Náměstí Republiky*

Evidently the first completed building in Prague with façades in true Secession style, it maintains consistent symmetry, emphasizing the central axis by a gently arched oriel. Characteristic is the ornamental glass cornice below a decorative gable. The original Secession hotel ball room was rebuilt in the twenties and now serves as a theatre.

|42|
Wilson Train Station

1901-09
Josef Fanta
1: Nové Město, Wilsonova ulice
metro C: *Hlavní nádraží*

While the architect won the competition with a Neo-Renaissance design, the actual building belongs already to the Secession. It has a dominant vestibule on a semicircular plan, with a high vault, and a large semicircular window. The latter is symmetrically abutted by two slim towers with allegorical figures. Two low-slung wings open up from the central section, terminated by higher pavilions. The platforms are covered by a steel two-aisle atrium. In the early 70s a new departure hall was built in front of the historical building. The expressway passing along its roof, elevated somewhat the original level of the terrain.

143

U Nováků House

1901-04

Osvald Polívka

1: Nové Město, Vodičkova 28

metro A, B: Můstek; streetcar 3, 9, 14, 24: Václavské náměstí

The first full-service department store in Prague, modelled on Parisian examples, connected to adjacent edifices by arcades. Built in full-blown Secession style, its main façade is decorated by a mosaic with an allegory of Commerce and Industry, designed by J. Preisler.

144

Insurance Company "Praha"

1903-05

Osvald Polívka

1: Staré Město, Národní 7

streetcar 9, 18, 22: Národní divadlo

Together with the next door Topičů House it represents an example of a richly decorative Secession façade. The portal is severely symmetrical with a massive central oriel. The windows are set between consoles under a radically extended cornice, and flanked by the letters of the company marquee "Praha", rendered in relief. The sculptures and reliefs are the work of Ladislav Šaloun.

145

Hotel Europa (Archduke Steven)

1903-05

Quido Bělský, Bedřich Bendelmayer, Bohumil Hypšman, Jan Letzel

1: Nové Město, Václavské náměstí 25

metro A, B: Můstek

An ensemble of two opulently decorated Secession buildings, of which the larger has highly arched windows in the ground floor café, with an entresol and a decorative marquee above the main entrance. The interior of the café has been preserved in its High Secession style.

146
The House of the Hlahol Choir
1903-06
Josef Fanta
1: Nové Město, Masarykovo nábřeží 16
metro B: Palackého náměstí; streetcar 17: Jiráskovo náměstí

As part of a coherent line of the eclectic buildup along the embankment, the house is remarkable for its delicate Secession façade, which discloses direct influence of both the Viennese and French Secession. The arched central gable is decorated by a mosaic painting of Music by K. Mottl; the façade has a relief by J. Pekárek.

147
Community House of the Capital City of Prague
1903-12
Antonín Balšánek, Osvald Polívka
1: Staré Město, Náměstí Republiky 5
metro B; streetcar 5, 14, 26: Náměstí Republiky

A distinctive edifice built in the Secession style from the competition winner's design. Its dis-

position is diagonally symmetrical, developed around the central ballroom and concert hall with a capacity of 1,500 people. The hall is lined with a promenade and, along the circumference of the building, with a wreath of subsidiary halls, richly decorated by paintings and sculptures. Above the entrance portico is a wide balcony, which connects to the Lord Mayor's Salon, with interior painted by Alfons Mucha.

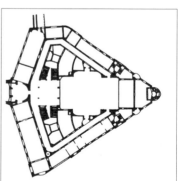

148
House of publisher Topič
1907-08
Osvald Polívka
1: Staré Město, Národní 9
streetcar 9, 18, 22: *Národní divadlo*

A Secession style façade decorates the building, already equipped with ferroconcrete ceilings. It has a well developed appointment of public spaces; to the store was added an exhibition hall in the basement and a plastic arts salon on the ground floor behind the store.

149
Laichter's House
1908-09
Jan Kotěra
2: Vinohrady, Chopinova 4
metro A: *Náměstí Jiřího z Poděbrad*

Just as the architect's own villa, this residence is the harbinger of modern rational architecture. Its façade is segmented in cubic volumes, which correspond to the usage of the interior spaces. The piano nobile is accentuated by a massive oriel, while the varied bonding of the brickwork provides the only ornamentation of the surface.

150
Villa of the Architect Jan Kotěra
1908-09
Jan Kotěra
10: Vinohrady, Hradešínská 8
metro A: *Náměstí Jiřího z Poděbrad*

The very modest resolution of the building marks the arrival of rational architecture. The building is divided into three vertically escalated right-angled volumes; the largest is covered by a low pyramidal roof. The slim entrance tower has a flat surface, as does the lowest part of the garden wing. The façades are unadorned, with emphasis on the composition of the windows in the wall surfaces.

151

Štenc's House
1909-11
Otakar Novotný
1: Josefov, Salvátorská ulice 8
metro A: *Staroměstská*

A residential house with a graphic studio and printing shop, built for the photographer and publisher Jan Štenc. One of the most conspicuous buildings of the so-called Individualistic Modernism. It shows almost complete eradication of any ornamental elements from the façade, with only the structure of rough brickwork remaining. It is alternately red and white, the latter found in the expressively important places (the pillars segmenting the ground floor). The geometric pattern of the white bricks articulates the entrance vestibule and stairway. Windows are used to divide the façade, differentiated by size and shape according to the interior arrangement and purpose of the rooms. The residential floor has a massive circular balcony, while on the top floor the house is enclosed by the rounded windows of the photographic studio.

152

Villa of the Sculptor František Bílek
1910-11
František Bílek
1: Hradčany, Mickiewiczova 1
metro A: *Hradčanská*

The sculptor built his "sculptural" house on a prominent site in the vicinity of the Prague Castle. On the intersection of two streets lies a circularly arched brick building, whose façade is fronted by heavy Egyptian columns shaped in concrete, which carry terraces placed at different heights and outline a monumental gallery.

153
The House at the Black Mother of Our Lord
1911-12
Josef Gočár
1: Staré Město, Ovocný trh 19
metro B; streetcar 5, 14, 26: Náměstí Republiky

The six-story building has a subtle ferroconcrete frame, allowing for a maximally lightened façade with large windows. The capitals of the interfenestral pillars are distinctly Cubist, as are the portal, grillwork, and railings. The actual height of the building is suppressed by a two-story mansard roof, with cubistically framed dormers. Following reconstruction in 1994, the house is now the Museum of Czech Cubism.

154
The Urbánek House (Mozarteum)
1911-12
Jan Kotěra
1: Nové Město, Jungmannova ulice 31
metro A, B: Můstek

One of the first buildings of modern architecture in Prague is a residental house with a shop and a theatre, outlined by a distinctive concrete frame, and capped by a high triangular gable. The ground floor is maximally open by display windows, the pillars are decorated with statues by Jan Štursa, the upper floors of rough bricks are articulated by lesenes, which become more numerous in the upward direction.

155
Triplex House
1912-13
Josef Chochol
2: Vyšehrad, Rašínovo nábřeží 6-10
streetcar 3, 7, 17: Výtoň

A symmetrical composition of three three-story dwellings. The central house has a distinctive entrance portal, with an oriel and tympanum; the lateral buildings have side entrances, tucked under open-work oriels. Above the first floor with dynamically bevelled intrafenestral walls is a richly modelled cornice, with Cubist curvatures. Placed above this is a mansard roof with massively framed angled dormers.

156
The Kovařovic Villa
1912-13
Josef Chochol
2: Vyšehrad, Libušina ulice 49
streetcar 3, 7, 17: Výtoň

One of Prague's most radical Cubist buildings is a family villa wedged between two other edifices built at the same time. All four façades are angled and facetted. On the entrance side it has a massively extended cornice, while the garden-side façade is dominated by a large curved oriel with a terrace. The top-floor windows are massively framed in a dormer-like arrangement. The Cubist ornamentation is evident in the plan of the garden, as well as the posts and bars of the fencing.

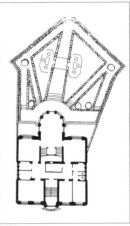

157
The Borough of Dejvice
1921-24 (the comprehensive plan)
Antonín Engel
metro A: Dejvická

Dejvice became a part of Prague in 1923, and a comprehensive plan was created for it. It was to be the only grandiosely conceived residential district with a central square at the intersection of three wide radially configured boulevards. It was planned to have wide streets, green courtyards within residential blocks, and houses with an unified, traditional expression; this concept was also consistently applied to public buildings. Only in the Thirties did Functionalism find its way into the borough.

158
Tenement House
1913-14
Josef Chochol
2: Vyšehrad, Neklanova 30
streetcar 7, 18, 24: *Na slupi*
A dwelling in the style of Radical Cubism with a slim continuous pillar on the corner leaving a Gothic impression, a cubistically expressive open-work crest cornice, and the whole exterior façade delicately facetted. The courtyard façade is smooth; the entrance vestibule with an open-work soffit is Cubist, as are the door handles on the main door.

159
Law Faculty of the Charles University
(1914) 1921-31
Jan Kotěra, Ladislav Machoň
1: Josefov, Náměstí Curieových 7
metro A: *Staroměstská*; streetcar 17: *Právnická fakulta*
Only half of a grandiose plan to turn part of the embankment into an university quarter was realized. The building is kept within the spirit of Traditionalism, having a monumental portico and a high gable, with Cubist reminiscences in its decor. The inner hall with galleries and overhead lighting is already strictly Purist.

160
Three Residences
1919-21
Otakar Novotný
1: Staré Město, ulice Elišky Krásnohorské 10-14
metro A: *Staroměstská*
A trio of houses of very elegant Cubist expression; it has rich plastic articulation with alternating oriels, emphasized cornices, and distinctive triangular attic gables. Unlike earlier Cubist edifices, here the articulation of the surfaces of the façades is underscored by various coloration.

161
Bank of the Czechoslovak Legionaires
1921-1923
Josef Gočár
1: Nové Město, Na Poříčí 24
metro B: Náměstí Republiky; streetcar 3, 24: Bílá labut'

An important building in the new form of Cubism, which evolved in the early twenties as the so-called National Style, or Rondocubism. The shapes are rounded and give a more massive and dynamic impression. Correlations with the House of the Black Mother of Our Lord can be seen in the façade: tripartite bay windows inserted into whole sections of the concrete-framed construction, similar ochre and red coloration. The plastic decoration is enhanced by capitals with reliefs of Jan Štursa and a frieze by Otto Gutfreund above the second floor. Inside, at the end of a long arcade, is an extensive bank hall with a glazed triple barrel vault. František Kysela participated in the interior decoration. The second stage of the Legionaires' Bank, a supremely Functionalist building by František Marek from 1937-39, attaches directly to the Rondocubist structure. It contains an uncluttered arcade with shops, cafés, and a basement-level theatre.

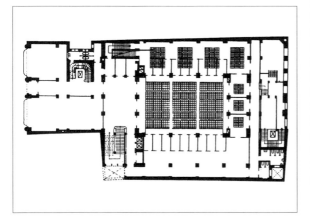

162
The Former Military Geographical Institute
1921-25
Bedřich Feuerstein
6: Bubeneč, Rooseweltova 23
metro A: Dejvická

The strict, somewhat austere, Cubist building represents the efforts to create a new Purist style with reference to Classicism and Empire. The only expressive elements consist of massive, seemingly doubled interfenestral pillars and squarely articulated parapets; the only adornment of the closed mass consists of the corner niches with sculptures.

163

Adria Palace (Insurance Company Riunione Adriatica di Sicurtà)
1922-25
Pavel Janák, Josef Zasche
1: Nové Město, Jungmannova 31
metro A, B: Můstek

A monumental, heavy building in the Rondocubist style, resolved in the spirit of an Ital-ian Renaissance palace with two tall massive towers on the two upper-most floors. The interfenestral elements and suprafenestral frontons contain rich plastic decoration, with reliefs by Otto Gutfreund between the large first-floor windows, and a bronze plastic of Adria by Jan Štursa above the fifth floor on the façade towards Národní třída. A curved arcade with shops and a theatre passes through the palace.

164

Residential House
1923-25
Otakar Novotný
7: Holešovice, Kamenická ulice 35
streetcar 1, 8, 25, 26: Kamenická

The house stands out in the otherwise ordinary development of the street by its robustly articulated façade, with heavy advanced cylindrical pillars on the ground floor, massive semicylindrical interfenestral pillars, and semicircular cornices turned alternately up (above the pillars), and down (below the windows). The last floor, above the protruding cornice, is smooth, with only the vaulted windows piercing the entire arched ornamention of the façade.

165
Water Purification Plant
1923-28
Antonín Engel
4: Podolí, Podolská 17
streetcar 3, 17: Podolská vodárna
An emphatic example of strict enforcement of Neo-Classicist procedures, regardless of the purpose of the building. The water plant is approached as a monumental palace building, with a high order of pilasters and plastically terminated attics. Its southern part was built in similar style in the 1950s.

166
Avion Palace (today Letka)
1924-26
Bohumír Kozák
1: Nové Město, Václavské náměstí 41
metro C: Muzeum; A, B: Můstek
The house with the first Proto-Functionalist façade in the centre of Prague. A long arcade leads through the ground floor. It is lined with shops and restaurants, with a cinema in the basement. On the first floor is a café with an extended, oriel-like, framed glassed wall. On the upper floors are offices with windows arranged in an almost continuous belt. The upper-most residential floors are recessed behind two terraces.

167
Reconstruction of the Town Square below Emauzy
1923-31
Bohumil Hypšman
2: Nové Město, Palackého náměstí
metro B: Karlovo náměstí

In 1907 a public competition was announced for the adaptation of the vacant space on the embankment below the Emauzy monastery. The construction was realized only in the twenties, when an ensemble of ministerial buildings was erected, emphasizing the axial view of the monastery and evoking the impression of strict symmetry. The buildings maintain a traditional character with a classical repertory of columns, pylons, pergolas, obeliscs, and slanted ridge-tiled roofs.

168

Masaryk's Social Institution (presently the Thomayer Hospital)
1924-40
Bohumír Kozák
4: Krč, Thomayerova 4
bus 106, 113, 114, 134, 139, 170: Thomayerova nemocnice

An extensive precinct consisting of free-standing three and four-story pavilions expressively Purist, laid out symmetrically in five parallel rows around a central oblong plaza, lined by a pergola. In the second half of the 1930s the Insitute for the Needs of Mother and Child was built nearby. Already a purely Functionalist building with plain surfaces, a pronounced elegant window graphic in the facing of the façade, and uncluttered interior composition. Functionalism manifests itself here as an independent mature style.

169

City Library
1924-28
František Roith
1: Josefov, Mariánské náměstí 1
metro A: Staroměstská

An example of traditional architecture, conceived as Classicist, with strict symmetrical composition. It has distinctive corner buttresses with a pillared arcade and a shallow portico, terminated by sculptural decorations. Its public character is emphasized by the granite slabs lining the exterior. Art-Deco style ornamentation adorns the interior walls and ceilings.

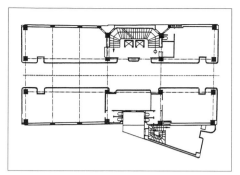

170
Lindt Department Store (today Astra)
1925-27
Ludvík Kysela
1: Nové Město, Václavské náměstí 4
metro A, B: *Můstek*

One of the first modern commercial palaces in the centre of Prague with a typical layout: on the ground floor an arcade lined with shops; on the floors above, cafés, shops, and offices for rent; on the highest levels apartments and an architect's studio. It has a light ferroconcrete-frame structure and a transparent glass façade (the current appearance is due to the inappropriate adaptation from the mid-70s). The last floor is terminated by a lofty curve of rounded windows.

171
Edison Transformer Station
1926-30
František Albert Libra
2: Nové Město, Jeruzalémská 2
streetcar 3, 5, 9, 14, 24: *Jindřišská*

A small, but massive looking building of purely technical character, with bands of horizontally segmented windows. It is a fine example of a cultivated Functionalist solution for this type of structure. Libra approached industrial and technical buildings programmatically. In the 1930s it contained a kinetic neon-light plastic by Zdeněk Pešánek.

119

172
Trade Exhibition Palace
1926-28
Oldřich Tyl, Josef Fuchs
7: Holešovice, Třída Dukelských hrdinů
47
metro C: *Vltavská*; streetcar 5, 12, 17: *Strossmayerovo náměstí*

The great mass of the first Functionalist building in Prague represents only a quarter of the intended trade exhibition precinct as it was proposed in the 1924 competition. The exterior appearance is very severe; the building is divided into two unequal parts–the southern has strip windows, the northern has square industrial windows, set in bare walls. The interior contains the grandiose spaces of two halls–the so-called Great Hall, formerly the Engineering Hall, and the so-called Little Hall, whose central space, with a glass skylight, is circled by six levels of galleries. The construction is concrete-frame, quite sophisticated for its time. The building was almost destroyed by fire in 1974; it was reconstructed from designs of M. Masák in 1980-1995. The reconstruction preserved the spatial conception, but the bearing elements had to be reinforced and they lost their original lightness.

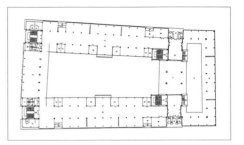

120

173

Alfa Palace (Stýblo)
1927-29
Ludvík Kysela
1: Nové Město, Václavské náměstí 28
metro A, B: Můstek; streetcar 3, 9, 14, 24: *Václavské náměstí*

A typical Prague palace of the 1920's with shops and cafés on the first two floors, concentrated around an interior arcade with a glass-concrete vault. The upper floors held rental office space, while the basement housed a cinema.

The main façade is unusually divided by two massive buttresses, which are terminated on the top floor by high glassed walls. The façade has continuous bands of minimally segmented windows with pivoting upper portions. The arcade exits into the Franciscan Garden and is connected at a right angle to the adjacent Světozor Arcade.

174

Bata Department Store (House of Services)
1927-29
Design Department of the Bata Corporation, in collaboration with Ludvík Kysela
1: Nové Město, Václavské náměstí 6
metro A, B: Můstek

The prototypical Bata Department Store, comprising seven floors with a concrete-frame construction in traditional modules of 6.15 meters with round pillars, and a maximally glazed outer shell. Only narrow bands of the faces of the ceiling slabs pierce the façade. On the front façade bands of white opaque glass were used as brackets for advertising signs. These were fabricated to work also under nightly lighting conditions. The original access was from the arcade, tied into the Lindt House next door; additional commercial spaces were located in the basement.

175
Hotel Juliš
1927-30
Pavel Janák
1: Nové Město, Václavské náměstí 22
metro A, B: Můstek

The hotel is built on a characteristically narrow Gothic lot. Its front tract is a purely Functionalist tall slim building. The façade has strip windows with opaque glass, alternating with white parapets, while the side loggias emphasize the slimness of the whole composition. A traditional pastry shop curves round the deep hallway, leading to an underground cinema. The first two floors contain a large hall and a glass-enclosed two-story café with a rounded gallery.

176
Church of St. Wenceslas
1927-30
Josef Gočár
10: Vršovice, náměstí Svatopluka Čecha
streetcar 4, 6, 22: Čechovo náměstí

The project won a public competition. The church is made of ferroconcrete, built on a slope in the middle of a square. It opens up above a wide staircase, in the middle of which rises a slim tower, practically of industrial character. Behind it the mass of the church rises gradually, synchronously with the terrain, up to the semicircular choir, which is lightened by tall windows. The interior space is open, with a deep choir gallery above the entrance.

177
The House of the Association of Figurative Artists Mánes
1927-30
Otakar Novotný
1: Nové Město, Masarykovo nábřeží 1-250
streetcar 17: Jiráskovo náměstí

It was built between the embankment and the southern tip of the island of Žofín. The lightweight building, vaulted over several piers, spans a shoulder of the Vltava and creates a light horizontal footing to the dark Gothic water tower. It represents the emotive side of Functionalism, quite rare in Czech architecture. The original interior articulation directed the exhibition spaces towards the embankment. The restaurant was ori-

ented onto the terraces facing the island, while the meeting rooms were in the basement above the river, and the offices on the first floor.

178
Ministry of Transportation
1927-31
Antonín Engel
1: Nové Město, Nábřeží Ludvíka Svobody 12
metro B, C: *Florenc*

A heavy, monumental building in Neo-Classicist style sits on a solid plinth with plastically lined stones, articulated by a high order of pilasters. It is topped with a stepped roof, whose attic is in the corners of the lateral wings accentuated by heavy figurative plastics. It is an example of Historicism, used on official national edifices even during the period of mature Functionalism.

179
Muller's Villa
1928-30
Adolf Loos, Karel Lhota
6: Střešovice, Nad hradním vodojemem 14
streetcar 1, 2, 18: *Ořechovka*

A tightly closed block with minimal, sharply carved out window openings, represents on the interior a masterly example of Loos's "Raumplan". The traditional division into floors is abandoned, the spaces penetrate each other, and line up in a spiral along stairways. The open walls offer views and visual connection on the individual levels. Expensive materials are used on the interior, with the characteristic patterns of wood and stone. The terrace on the flat roof is bordered by a concrete frame, outlining the view of the Castle panorama.

180

Residential Ensemble Baba
1928-33
Pavel Janák (regulatory plan)
6: Dejvice; Na ostrohu, Na Babě, Nad
Pat'ankou, Matějská
bus 125, 131: U Matěje

The model colony Baba was created on the behest of the Association for Czechoslovak Achievement as a permanent exhibition of a new life style: healthy living in family homes with modern architectural solutions. In the original plan 30 houses were projected, built on parallel streets on a hillside, guaranteeing everyone a similar unobstructed view of the valley of the Vltava river. The houses were designed by lead-

ing Functionalist architects, for instance J. Gočár, O. Starý, J.E. Koula, A. Heythum, E. Linhart, H. Kučerová-Záveská, A. Benš, A. Černý, as well as the Dutch architect Mart Stamm. The houses were designed to suit their middle-class inhabitants, who were architects, creative artists, publishers, etc. The houses have ferroconcrete constructions, maximally open ground plans, strip windows, and spacious terraces. The last of the houses were built in the forties, respecting the original intentions of the model colony.

181

Restaurant and Terraces at Barrandov
1929
Max Urban
5: Hlubočepy, Barrandovská 1
bus 105, 192, 246, 247, 248: Barrandovské terasy

In 1927 Max Urban worked out a regulatory plan of a new villa district in the area of Barrandov.
At the northern headland of the territory he placed a picturesque amphitheatre of observation terraces, which carefully follows the shape of the terrain. This is terminated by a delicate restaurant pavilion, crowned by a high tower. The building is typically Functionalist: light, transparent, with large windows, marquees,

pergolas, and an arbour. The terraces are outlined by low stone walls, which give the ensemble an expression of organic architecture, in harmony with nature.

182
Church of the Holiest Heart of Our Lord
1928-32
Josip Plečnik
2: Vinohrady, Náměstí Jiřího z Poděbrad
metro A: Náměstí Jiřího z Poděbrad
In the middle of a park rises a sacral building, uncommon in Prague, inspired by Early Christian architecture. The cube of the cathedral hall is built on a plan of 26 × 38 meters, with height of 13 meters. Its exterior is faced to the height of the diagonally placed cornice. It has vitrified brick with regularly spaced stone protrusions; its upper part is covered with snow-white plaster. Across the whole width rises a glazed tower lined with pylons and obelisks, 42 meters high.

183
Palace of the Municipal Transportation Company, previously the Electric Company of the Capital City of Prague
1928-1936
Adolf Benš, Josef Kříž
7: Holešovice, Bubenská 1
metro C; streetcar 1, 3, 8, 14, 25: Vltavská
The palace, built on a cruciform plan, began as one of Prague's first comprehensively equipped modern administrative buildings. The central part is eight-storied with an interior-gallery atrium to its full height, a glass roof, and six-story side wings. The complex has a compact three-floor base, which levels out the uneven terrain. The ground floor contains shops, the basement has

a concert hall, and a medical facility is located in the western wing. The ferroconcrete frame construction has a module of 5.20 × 5.20 meters. Characteristic is the white ceramic facing of the façade.

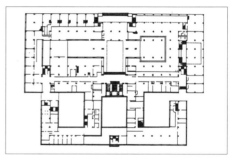

184
Barrandov Film Studios
1931-34
Max Urban
5: Barrandov, Kříženeckého náměstí 5
bus 105, 192, 246, 247, 248: Filmové ateliéry
The large four-story building on a U-shaped plan overlooks a plaza. It has rows of large windows and is dominated by a staircase tower, topped by a water tower. Behind the administrative and

operations building two studio halls extend towards the rear, each of them on a plan of 20 × 32 meters. The patented system of dry stone walling with large blocks was used in their construction. The area gradually grew to include more production pavilions. It is still used to produce films.

185
Department Store with the "Black Rose" Arcade
1929-32
Oldřich Tyl
1: Nové Město, Panská 4
metro A, B: Můstek; streetcar 3, 9, 14, 24: Václavské náměstí
The department store with rental office space filled an empty lot in Panská Street with characteristic Functionalist architecture. It shows large, geometrically articulated windows, and a plain façade. Deep into the lot is a three-story gallery, encompassing an atrium crowned with a glass and concrete barrel vault. The walkways of the gallery are made of glass and concrete blocks, and are extended on refined concrete cantilevers. The arcade passes perpendicularly through a small courtyard, allowing access to the courtyard garden, and leads all the way to the Neo-Renaissance palace, At the Black Rose, which opens onto the boulevard Na Příkopě. The current appearance is from the early sixties, when an open bi-brachial circular winding staircase was added, and the graceful Functionalist lighting figures were removed.

186
General Pension Institute (today House of the Trade Unions)
1929-34
Josef Havlíček, Karel Honzík
3: Žižkov, Náměstí W. Churchilla 2
metro C: Hlavní nádraží; streetcar 2, 9, 26: Husinecká

The project resulted from a competition, in which it was the only submission to disregard the mandated resolution in the form of a closed city block. It suggested instead a free-standing cruciform disposition with the separate wings of the administrative section being of different heights, complemented by low lateral wings with rental apartments and shops. Its façades are plain, faced with white ceramic tiles, with carefully calculated proportions between the areas of wall space and areas of paired square windows. The first modern skyscraper in Prague, it was also its first fully air-conditioned building. Its distinctness and purity made it for a long time a prime symbol of mature Czech Functionalism.

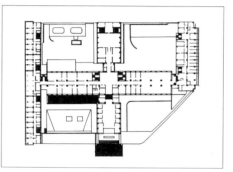

187
Former French School
1931-34
Jan Gillar
6: Dejvice, Bílá 1
metro A: Dejvická

On the basis of an architectural competition an ensemble of school buildings was erected, divided according to their use into individual pavilions and self-contained blocks. Independently accessible are the kindergarden and gymnasium pavilions, with a theatrical hall on the top floor. This is connected to the main school buildings by a covered walkway. The exterior with the variously shaped windows reflects its functional purpose. It is an expression of the so-called scientific stream in Functionalist architecture, maintaining nonetheless a very rich total colourful composition.

188
Prague Airport at Ruzyň
1932-34
Adolf Benš
6: Ruzyň, K letišti 2
bus 108, 119, 179: *Staré letiště*

The new Prague airport corresponded with the most advanced demands of air traffic at the time of construction, and its appearance reflected the dynamism of the fast evolving mode of transportation.

The centre of the customer-handling area consists of the airport vestibule with a softly curved vaulted roof; the symmetrical, plain, two-story side wings have a strictly ordered layout of windows.

Dominant is the control tower with lightweight galleries and a roof-top terrace.

The guardhouse at the airport entrance is the work of Kamil Roškot from 1934-35.

189
The House of the Arts and Crafts Industry
1934-35
Oldřich Starý
1: Nové Město, Národní třída 36-38
metro B: *Národní třída*; A, B: *Můstek*

A commercial and office building with a basement exhibition hall. It lies on a L-shaped lot, and has on the ground floor a shopping mall with gently rounded corners, and a retractable glass roof. The exterior façades are maximally opened with only minimal bands of ceiling structures. The segmentation of the glass surfaces corresponds to the functional purpose of differentiating the shops and the offices. On the upper floors the plain volume recedes behind two terraces. It represents an excellent example of functionally pure expression.

190
Commercial Palace Merkur
1934-36
Jaroslav Fragner
1: Staré Město, Revoluční 25
streetcar 5, 14, 26: *Dlouhá třída*

The monumental volume of the seven-story palace creates a ceremonial entrance from the embankment to Revoluční Street, descending with five floors along the street. It uses traditional Functionalist vocabulary of symmetrically spaced wide windows, with maximal glazing of the ground and first floors, including elegantly rounded shop windows. Under the frontal high buttress it places a light balcony, forming a tall entrance niche. However, by the use of heavy stone facing and by emphasizing dignity and prestige, it moves closer to the Classicist tradition, and away from Functionalist lightness, which was highly prized at the time.

191
Sevastopol Palace
1937-39
Antonín Černý, Bohumír Kozák
1: Staré Město, Na Příkopě 31
metro B: *Náměstí Republiky*

The palace of the insurance company Assicurazioni Generali e Moldavia Generali, is a commercial and residential building, with a cinema in the basement, and an arcade winding through two inner courtyards. These are roofed with glass-concrete vaults. In three tracts were offices and apartments with variable layouts. The exterior appearance of the palace is geometrically very disciplined, with an even arrangement of windows, cut into the stone façade of the street-side, and with ceramic facing on the courtyard side. The arcade was lined with elegant shop windows framed in stainless steel and with rounded glass panes.

192
The White Swan Department Store
1937-39
Josef Hrubý, Josef Kittrich
1: Nové Město, Na poříčí 23
metro B, C: Florenc; streetcar 3, 24: Bílá labut'

The first full-service department store in Prague was built following a design competition. The ground floor was proposed as an open urban mall with display columns. The shoppers slow-ly pass by them on their way to shopping areas. The latter covers five stories, with a suspended light-weight glass façade, segmented into a square grid. The office and communal facilities were concentrated within the rooftop additions: the first recedes behind a narrow terrace, while the other forms a two-story tower with strip windows and an extended sunny pergola. The whole composition is crowned by a revolving neon symbol of a white swan.

193
Hotel Jalta
1953-55
Antonín Tenzer
1: Nové Město, Václavské náměstí
metro A, C: Muzeum; A, B: Můstek

The hotel was built on one of the lots in the centre of the city, made available after the Second World War. It is one of the few buildings in the style known as Socialist Realism. Rather than historicizing, it is closer to being decorative, with a heavy travertine façade, distinctive geometrical ornamentation on the stone balustrades of the balconies and on the metalwork of the windows. On the first two floors it has partly opened café terraces, uncommon in Prague.

194
Hotel International
1953-59
František Jeřábek
6: Podbaba, Náměstí Družby
streetcar 20, 25: Podbaba

One of the most characteristic buildings of so-called Socialist Realism period in Prague. Inspired by the Historicism practiced in Soviet architec-

ture, it was originally designed as a hostelry for soldiers, but reworked during construction into a luxury hotel. It has a rigorous symmetrical composition with a central dominant of a stepped tower. This is, however, diminished by the fact that the building is located on an insignificant square in a valley. The interiors preserve period relief works and elements of decorative arts and crafts.

131

195

Restaurant Praha EXPO '58
1958, in Prague 1960
František Cubr, Josef Hrubý, Zdeněk Pokorný
7: Letná, Skalecká
streetcar 5, 12, 14, 17, 26: Nábřeží kapitána Jaroše
At the World Fair EXPO '58 in Brussels, Czech architecture introduced itself with a pavilion which indicated the definitive abandonment of Socialist Realism and announced the return to modern architecture. The pavilion was a great success and received the Gold Medal for architecture and for the exhibition as a whole; the pavilion was brought back to Prague. It was divided into two buildings: the exhibition part was installed in Stromovka Park, but it burnt down

in 1991; the restaurant section was placed at the edge of the Letná Plain, with an excellent view of the city. It has a subtle steel structure, maximally glazed walls, and it opens up over Prague in a delicately arched circle. It has been under reconstruction since 1994.

196

The Institute of Macromolecular Chemistry of the Czech Academy of Sciences
1960-63
Karel Prager
6: Petřiny, Heyrovského náměstí
streetcar 1, 2, 18: Petřiny
After the World Fair EXPO '58 in Brussels, Czech architecture regained its rational and constructive spirit. A period of intensive growth began, with use of new materials and construction techniques. The Institute represents one of the most important buildings of the period. It is the first to introduce the composition of a low broad footing and a perpendicular tall slim slab; it also pioneers the use of new lightweight suspension pan-

els of aluminum and glass. In the coming years both were repeated so often, that the originally attractive architectural form turned prosaic.

197

Acquatic Stadium at Podolí
1959-64
Richard Podzemný, Gustav Kuchař, Juraj Domič
4: Podolí, Podolská 74
streetcar 3, 17: Kublov
The complex was built on the site of a former quarry on the banks of the Vltava. On the street-side it is terminated by the hall containing the covered pool, with steeply vaulted ferroconcrete asymmetrical circular frames of the roof structure, while on the other side of a terrace it ends with an adjacent free-standing pavilion of the summer changing rooms. In a sheltered area protected by a high cliff are three pools (50 meters, 33 meters, and a chil-

dren's pool), with the roof of the hall forming a grandstand for spectators. To date it is the only facility in Prague with a 50 meter indoor pool.

132

198

Hotel Intercontinental

1968-73

Karel Filsak, Karel Bubeníček, Jaroslav Švec; Jan Šrámek, František Cubr (interiors); Karel Koutský (reconstruction)

1: Josef, Náměstí Curieových 5

streetcar 17: Právnická fakulta

One of the first examples of new architecture entering directly into the historical core of the city; simultaneously one of the earliest examples of conspicuous application of fair-faced concrete in Czech architecture. The richly articulated ground plan responds to the street grid and to the need to create an intimate park space, separated from the heavily travelled embankment. The main part, which has seven floors, is gradually reduced to five.

Massive concrete volumes separate the common ground floor area from the hostelry section; at the top the sightseeing restaurants form the crown. In 1993-95 the hotel was rebuilt, especially its interiors, and a high-tech fitness centre was added.

199

Tower of the Church at Emauzy

1963-67

František Maria Černý

2: Nové Město, Na Slovanech

metro B: Karlovo náměstí

At the end of the Second World War during the bombing of Prague, the Gothic towers of the convent at Emauzy were destroyed. In the late 50s and early 60s two rounds of architectural competitions for their renovation were held. Amidst designs based mostly on a historical arrangement of the mass, one totally different concept stood out. It presented modern twin towers consisting of a ferroconcrete shell, in a remarkably dynamic, upwardly extended form.

200

Máj Department Store (K-Mart)
1973-75
John Eisler, Miroslav Masák,
Martin Rajniš
1: Nové Město, Národní
třída 26
metro B; streetcar 6, 9, 18, 22: Národní
třída

Máj was built as the third full-service department store in Prague, intended primarily for everyday shopping. This corresponds with its simple, almost rough shaping with only minimal plasticity. According to the design, the plain front façade was to be used as a changeable advertising surface, without much relationship to its historical surroundings. Emphasis is placed on easy orientation within the building. This is why the vertical access routes are placed into a separate, glassed hall-arcade on the southern side. This is an example of the terse, 'designer' approach to architecture, which was typical of the work of the architectural studio SIAL in Liberec, in the early 70s.

201

The Administrative Building of ČKD Industries Na můstku
1976-81
Jan Šrámek, Alena Šrámková
1: Staré Město, Václavské náměstí, Na Příkopě 1
metro A, B: Můstek

The house was built on a vacant lot created in the early 70s during the building of the subway system. In its vocabulary and expression it brought an unusual reaction to global tendencies, considering its time, as well as a re-evaluation of the highest traditions of Czech Functionalism of the period between the world wars. Also unusual was the function of the rental administrative building with shops, cafés, and a terrace. It is remarkable for its sensitive composition in a complex urbanistic context, while remaining sober and almost pragmatically cool. As soon as it was completed, it became a symbol of the newly developing Neo-Functionalism in Czech architecture.

134

202
Hotel Hoffmeister
1991-94
Petr Keil
1: Malá Strana, Pod Bruskou 9

metro A; streetcar 12, 18, 22: *Malostranská*

Built on the site of previously demolished town houses, it repeats the original shape on the corner, while in depth it develops in a pavilion configuration around a courtyard terrace. It also incorporates the only preserved Classicist house. One of the rare examples of Postmodernism, emanating from the character of Baroque Prague, especially in the resolution of the mansard dormers, and the Atlas at the corner entrance.

203
Nová Scéna Lanterna Magica Theatre
1980-83
Karel Prager, Stanislav Libenský
1: Nové Město, Národní třída

streetcar 6, 9, 18, 22: *Národní divadlo*

During the 1960s several competions for the completion of the area of the National Theatre were held. Only at the end of the 70s did the reconstruction of the historical building and completion of the surroundings commence.

Originally a multipurpose cultural facility was to be built, facing Národní Boulevard, but in 1981 it was decided to build another theatrical building with the ability to change the stage configuration to either proscenium, Elizabethan, or arena-style. The complex acoustical requirements account for the building's heavy multilayered outer shell.

The Feal façade elements are faced with Cuban limestone, in front of which stands a wall of large-dimensional blown-glass elements. It is the first, and, so far only, example of collaboration between an architect and a glass artist on the resolution of monumental architecture in a demanding historical environment.

204

Office Centre Building

1992-94

Jiří Alda, Petr Dvořák, Martin Němec, Ján Štempel

2: Vinohrady, Římská 15

metro A, C: Muzeum

A typical example of the lively, developing tradition of Functionalism. A six-story sober volume with a rooftop addition behind a terrace and a regular network of similar windows in a cold stone facing, placed in an appropriate scale into the eclectic environment of town houses from the early 20th century. The high-placed glass marquee above the narrow entrance niche subscribes to the legacy of the

30s. Its interior arrangement develops in variable disposition around two glassed atrios.

205

"The Dancing House"

1992-96

Frank O. Gehry, Vlado Milunič

2: Nové Město, Rašinovo nábřeží 80

metro: B: Karlovo náměstí; streetcar 17: Jiráskovo náměstí

A rental office building encloses the block of an exposed streetcorner which was opened up at the end of War War II. Its dynamic architecture reacts to the complex location of the house within an assembly of Secession and eclectic buildings, whose even allignment it terminates by agitated curves used in both general resolution of its mass and in the placement of windows on each floor. Emphasis is on the shaping of the streetcorner, with two towers thrusting upwards. One is concrete, widening modestly as it rises. Attached to it is the other, made of glass. It is narrowed in the middle. The name "danc-

ing house" refers to the inspiration provided by the dance team of Ginger Rogers and Fred Astaire. The crown of the building is formed by a wire sculpture of the Medusa.

206
Local municipal offices of Praha–Řepy
1992-95
Jan Stašek, Zuzana Stašková
6: Řepy, Žalanského ulice
bus 225: *Místní úřad*

The formation of the pavilion building comes out of varied functional resolution: a closed quarter-round contains offices, a forward thrust raised point houses the Mayor's official areas, and the low garden-facing pavilion accomodates the meeting hall and wedding chambers. In its expression the building relates to the tradition of Functionalist architecture of the interwar period while simultaneously showing an inspiration by the "white" houses of Meier.

207
Pragobanka
1992-95
Radim Kousal
10: Strašnice, Vinohradská 230
metro A: *Strašnická*; streetcar 7, 11, 19, 26: *Vinice*

On the southern side the building faces the area of the prospective cultural centre by a modest wall which is undulated on the ground floor and in the receding roof extention in the rhythm of round pillars. At the corner it turns gently northwards into a deep entrance courtyard, which reflects on its mirrored walls an old house and a large tree. The courtyard is covered by a steeply pitched glass roof which serves as a panoramic focal point. The austerely elegant architecture maintains the tradition of Czech Neofunctionalism, enhanced by the expressive capabilities of technically precise materials and constructions.

208
Company of Computing Technology
1992-96
Jan Hančl
9: Libeň, Kovanecká 30
metro B: *Českomoravská*

One of the few new administrative buildings which almost deliberately does not wish to subscribe to the leading contemporary Neofunctionalist movement. It is nonetheless quite clearly inspired by naval vocabulary, including a "crow's nest" and a "bridge", which is included in the technical appointment of the building. The individual floors are layered in the manner of a transoceanic liner, with its soft curves intending the greatest possible illumination of the interiors. The western wall is distinctly different, in both its earthy coloration, and by its playful placement of irregular small window openings. The northern wall is shaped more modestly, with regular windows. It does, however, draw attention by its striking ochre colour.

Bibliography

General Interest

F. RUTH. Kronika Královské Prahy a obcí sousedních I-III. Prague. 1903-1904. (facsimile Prague. 1995).

Z. WIRTH. Zmizelá Praha, vols. 1-5. Prague. 1945-1948.

J. ČAREK, V. HLAVSA et all. Ulicemi Prahy. Prague. 1950.

Architektura v českém národním dědictví. Prague. 1961.

J. JANÁČEK. Malé dějiny Prahy. Prague. 1967.

J. HEROUT. Prahou deseti století. Prague. 1972.

V. HLAVSA. Praha očima staletí. Prague. 1972.

V. LORENC. Nové Město Pražské. Prague. 1973.

M. KORECKÝ. Praha v barevném reliéfu. Prague. 1975.

J. VANČURA. Hradčany. Pražský hrad. Prague. 1976.

E. POCHE, P. PREISS. Pražské paláce. Prague. 1977.

Ch. NORBERG-SCHULZ. Genius loci. London. 1981.

J. VANČURA, V. HLAVSA. Malá Strana. Prague. 1983.

E. POCHE. Prahou krok za krokem. Prague. 1985.

L. PETRÁŇOVÁ. Domovní znamení staré Prahy. Prague. 1988.

J. HRŮZA. Město Praha. Prague. 1989.

S. VODĚRA, J. STAŇKOVÁ, J. ŠTURSA. Pražská architektura, významné stavby jedenácti století. Prague. 1990.

O. BAŠEOVÁ. Pražské zahrady. Prague. 1991.

J. HILMERA. Pražská divadla / Theatres of Prague. Prague. 1995.

C. RYBÁR. Ulice a domy Prahy, Prague 1995.

YEARBOOKS Zprávy památkové péče.

YEARBOOKS Stoletá Praha.

Romanesque Architecture

K. FIALA. Pražsky hrad v době románské. Prague. 1933.

J. CIBULKA. Kostel sv. Jiří na hradě Pražském. Prague. 1936.

J. ČAREK. Kostel sv. Martina ve zdi. Prague. 1940.

J. ČAREK. Praha románská. Prague. 1947.

M. RADOVÁ. Architektura románská. Prague. 1972.

I. BORKOVSKÝ. Svatojiřská bazilika a klášter na Pražském hradě. Prague. 1975.

E. POCHE et all. Praha středověká,

Čtvero knih o Praze. Prague. 1983.

Gothic Architecture

V. BIRNBAUM. Chrám sv. Víta, Kniha o Praze I. Prague. 1930.

D. LÍBAL. Pražské gotické kostely. Prague. 1946.

Z. WIRTH. Pražský hrad ve středověku. Prague. 1946.

K. NOVOTNÝ, E. POCHE. Karlův most. Prague. 1947.

E. POCHE. Pražské portály. Prague. 1947.

D. LÍBAL. Gotická architektura v Čechách a na Moravě. Prague. 1948.

A. KUBIČEK. Betlémská kaple. Prague. 1953.

E. POCHE, J. KROFTA. Na Slovanech. Prague. 1956.

A. KUBIČEK, A. PETRÁŇOVÁ, J. PETRÁŇ. Karolinum a historické koleje University Karlovy v Praze. Prague. 1961.

G. FOEHR. Benedikt Ried. Munich. 1961.

B. NECHVÁTAL. Vyšehrad. Prague. 1970.

J. HEŘMAN, M. VILÍMKOVÁ. Pražské synagogy. Prague. 1970.

A. MERHAUTOVÁ. Raně středověká

architektura v Čechách. Prague. 1971.
J. Hořejší. Vladislavský sál Pražského hradu. Prague. 1973.
E. Poche et all. Praha středověká, Čtvero knih o Praze. Prague. 1983.
H. Soukupová. Anežský klášter v Praze. Prague. 1989.

Renaissance Architecture

O. Frejková. Palladianismus v české renesanci. Prague. 1949.
J. Krčálová. Centrální stavby české renesance. Prague. 1976.
E. Poche et all. Praha na úsvitu nových dějin, Čtvero knih o Praze. Prague. 1988.

Baroque Architecture

O. Stefan. Architektura, Pražské baroko. exhibition catalogue. Prague. 1938.
H.G. Franz. Bauten und Baumeister der Barockzeit in Bohmen. Lipsia. 1962.
J. Neumann. Český barok. Prague. 1974.
M. Pavlík, V. Uher. Dialog tvarů. Architektura barokní Prahy. Prague. 1974.
V. Kotrba. Česká barokní gotika. Dílo Jana Blažeje Santiniho. Prague. 1976.
V. Lorenc, K. Tříska. Černínský palác v Praze. Prague. 1980.
J. Sedlák. Jan Blažej Santini. Setkání baroku s gotikou. Prague. 1987.
E. Poche et all. Praha na úsvitu nových dějin, Čtvero knih o Praze. Prague. 1988.
Kilián Ignác Dientzenhofer a umělci jeho okruhu. Catalogue of the exhi-

bition at the Národní Galerie, Prague. 1989.

19th and 20th Century Architecture

100 let práce. Catalogue for the Jubilee Exhibition of the Kingdom of Bohemia. Prague. 1891.
Z. Wirth, A. Matějček. Česká architektura 19. století. Prague. 1922.
P. Janák. Sto let obytného domu nájemného v Praze. Prague. 1933.
A. Masaryková. Národní muzeum v Praze. Prague. 1940.
E. Krtilová. Architekt Josef Zítek. Prague. 1954.
V.V. Štech. Národní divadlo. Prague. 1954.
J. Zelinka. Pražská předměstí. Prague. 1956.
A. Javorin. Pražské arény. Prague. 1958.
H. Volavková. Židovské město pražské. Prague. 1959.
V. Mencl. Praha. Prague. 1969.
O. Nový. Architekti Praze. Prague. 1971.
J. Ehm, E. Poche. Pražské interiéry. Prague. 1973.
V. Šlapeta. Praha 1900-1978. Průvodce po moderní architektuře. Catalogue of the exhibition at the Prague Techinical Museum. Prague. 1978.
J. Vebr, O. Nový, R. Valterová. Soudobá architektura ČSSR. Prague. 1981.
J. Šnejdar et all. Národní divadlo. Prague. 1983.
M. Benešová. Česká architektura v proměnách dvou století. Prague. 1985.

R. Švácha. Od moderny k funkcionalismu. Prague. 1985.
Tschechische Kunst 1878-1914. Exhibition catalogue at the Matildenhohe. Darmstadt. 1984-85.
P. Wittlich. Umění a život doba secese. Prague. 1986.
J. Kohout, J. Vančura. Praha 19. a 20. století, technické proměny. Prague. 1986.
A. Moravánsky. Die Architektur der Donaumonarchie. Budapest. 1988.
R. Sedláková. Dům ČKD v Praze Na můstku. Catalogue of the exhibition at the J. Fragner Gallery. Prague. 1988.
Avantgarde und Tradition. Tchechische Kunst der 20er + 30er Jahre. Catalogue of the exhibition at the Mathildenhohe. Darmstadt. 1988-89.
E. Poche et all. Praha národního probuzení, Čtvero knih o Praze. Prague. 1980.
Z. Lukeš. Pražské vily / Prague villas. Prague. 1993.
R. Sedláková. Sorela — česká architektura padesátých let. Catalogue of the exhibition at the Národní Galerie in Prague. Prague. 1994.
J. Vybíral. Ignác Ullmann. Catalogue of the exhibition at the Národní Galerie. Prague. 1994.
Prague 1891-1941 Architecture and Design. Catalogue of the exhibition at the City Art Centre. Edinburg. 1994-95.
I. Margolius. A Guide to Twenties Century Architecture. Prague. London. 1994.
Praha kubistická / Cubistic Prague. Prague. 1995.

Index of places

*The names in small capital letters refer to those buildings covered at lenghth in this guide book. The **bold face** numbers refer to the numbering of the files, not the page number.*

Index of names